Young Turks and Kurds

A set of 'invisible' disadvantaged groups

Pinar Enneli, Tariq Modood and Harriet Bradley

JOSEPH ROWNTREE
FOUNDATION

The **Joseph Rowntree Foundation** has supported this project as part of its programme of research and innovative development projects, which it hopes will be of value to policy makers, practitioners and service users. The facts presented and views expressed in this report are, however, those of the authors and not necessarily those of the Foundation.

Joseph Rowntree Foundation
The Homestead
40 Water End
York YO30 6WP
Website: www.jrf.org.uk

First published 2005 by the Joseph Rowntree Foundation

ISBN 1 85935 273 1   (paperback)
ISBN 1 85935 274 X   (pdf: available at www.jrf.org.uk)

A CIP catalogue record for this report is available from the British Library.

Cover design by Adkins Design

Prepared and printed by:
York Publishing Services Ltd
64 Hallfield Road
Layerthorpe
York YO31 7ZQ
Tel: 01904 430033; Fax: 01904 430868; Website: www.yps-publishing.co.uk

Further copies of this report, or any other JRF publication, can be obtained either from the JRF website (www.jrf.org.uk/bookshop/) or from our distributor, York Publishing Services Ltd, at the above address.

Contents

Acknowledgements

This project would not have been possible without the participation of the young people and their families who generously gave us their time in completing questionnaires, in interviews and discussion groups, and in helping us in many ways. We are most grateful to them and to the community centres, sports clubs and coffee houses that assisted us in making contacts or gave us space to conduct meetings. We also thank those from local agencies and from the Haringey Council who were interviewed or who gave us advice and data. We are also grateful to our colleague, Dr David Shankland, for his comments on an early draft.

Throughout the study, we were assisted by an Advisory Group, which is listed below. We thank them for all the advice they gave us, especially the Chair, Charlie Lloyd of the Joseph Rowntree Foundation (JRF), for his detailed comments on the various drafts the report went through.

Project Advisory Group

- Prof. Haleh Afshar, University of York

- Dr Tehmina Basit, University of Leicester

- Prof. Gary Craig, University of Hull

- Kelami Dedezade

- Dr Mehmetali Dikerdem, Middlesex University

- Charlie Lloyd, Joseph Rowntree Foundation (Chair)

- Niyazi Uludag, Kurdish Advice Centre

Introduction

According to the 2001 census, 45 per cent of Britain's minority ethnic people live in London, where they comprise 29 per cent of all residents (www.statistics.gov.uk). Long-established minority groups, mainly settlers from the Commonwealth, such as those from the Caribbean or the Indian subcontinent, have been joined by more recent migrants: refugees from the countries of the former Yugoslavia or from trouble spots in sub-Saharan and North Africa. Britain's capital can truly be seen as a multicultural city at the centre of a new nexus of global movements. Yet, surprisingly little is known about many of Britain's smaller minority communities.

This research project looks at the position of young people within one such community grouping, London's Turkish speakers or those who have Turkish origins, which is concentrated particularly in the boroughs of Hackney and Haringey. This community is itself fragmented, comprising three main groups: Cypriot Turks, mainland Turks and Kurdish refugees.[1] However, there is a degree of intermarriage between these three groups and also with majority ethnic groups. This research focuses on a community that is characterised by complex interrelationships and that possesses commonalities in terms of its economic situation, culture, religion and external links with the global Turkish-speaking community. Very little research has explored the British component of the Turkish diaspora and, in particular, how young Turkish people are adapting to their lives in Britain (Enneli, 2001). This report presents some exploratory findings about the lives of London's young Turks and Kurds, including their ambitions and aspirations, and the choices and problems they face. It aims to give voice to the experiences of a group of young people who are largely invisible within youth research. In doing so, it seeks to contribute to our understanding of ethnic complexity and hybridity within an increasingly globalised culture and economy such as Britain.

Recent research has shown young people's transitions to adulthood to be increasingly fragmented, prolonged and unpredictable (Roberts, 1995; Furlong and Cartmel, 1997). The evidence points to increasing polarisation between well-qualified young people from privileged backgrounds and other groups that are increasingly disadvantaged and socially excluded. It is widely acknowledged that young people from minority ethnic backgrounds are likely to experience more disrupted transitions and to end up among the economically disadvantaged. For example, the Government's new youth programme, Connexions, identifies minority ethnic young people and asylum seekers and refugees as two of its targeted 'at risk' groups. At the same time, the changes in economic relations and the labour market are seen to be disrupting existing patterns of ethnic and gender segregation in the labour market, with some formerly disadvantaged groups (such as young Indian women) benefiting (Modood *et al.*, 1997; Walby, 1997). How are young Turks faring?

The answer to this question is unclear, because there remains an acute lack of research into the specific problems linked to the transitions of minority ethnic young people. In addition, many of these young people might be particularly hard to study as they are disproportionately represented among the Government's NEET category (not in employment, education or training). Britton *et al.* (2002) called these young people the 'disappeared', since they are not shown on records of the many agencies that deal with young people. Britton *et al.* (2002, p. 51) rightly point out that:

> The young 'disappeared' do exist ... And, sooner or later, they will probably be somebody's problem.

This research contributes to the exploration of such omissions and distortions, while focusing on the specific transitional experiences of a group we consider to be particularly disadvantaged: London's young Turks and Kurds.

The project explores how some of the most vulnerable segments of the younger generation of ethnic minorities experience the transition to adulthood, the important issues affecting them and their expectations and aspirations about their future prospects. It is now well established that, out of all of the minority groups commonly studied, the Bangladeshis are the most disadvantaged (Modood *et al.*, 1997), in terms of facility in English, educational qualifications, unemployment, occupational levels and earnings. However, evidence suggests that some Turkish-speaking groups are even more disadvantaged, even when they have been in Britain for a comparable period of time.

Our initial aim was to include Bangladeshi young people in our study as a comparative disadvantaged group. Unfortunately, despite considerable efforts, we were unable to reach our target number of Bangladeshi young people to enable a meaningful comparison. The details of our attempts to access the community can be seen in Appendix 2.

The core Turkish groups are chosen not just because their circumstances differ from those identified in mainstream youth research but also because they are missing from 'race' and minority ethnic research. This study not only explores processes of transition for minority ethnic youth, but also illuminates some of the complexities of ethnic identity today. Some of these complexities may be similar to those apparent more generally. For example, those associated with combinations and tensions between different sources of identity, such as religion and national origin, or – particularly true of young people – wanting to be associated with an ethnic group but not to be bound by its cultural practices (Modood *et al.*, 1994, 1997). Ethnic identities are complex and, while it is important that these issues inform policy, it is also important that generational and gender differences are properly appreciated and commonalities with other British peers are not obscured.

A key component of ethnic complexity in this research is the fact that Turks do not occupy a clear position in the white/non-white divide on which current understanding of 'ethnic minorities' is based. In the 1991 census, Turks, coming from the outer-edge of Europe, identified themselves as 'white'. Yet, Turkey is widely perceived in Britain to be a Third World, non-white country and Turks experience racial discrimination. By most measures of cultural difference, Turks are in a similar position to many non-white groups and in socio-economic terms are also more disadvantaged. This study, therefore, is an inquiry into how a 'white' group may be more disadvantaged than some 'non-white' groups, showing the error of correlating 'ethnic' with 'non-white'. Indeed, the very persistence of the 'white/non-white' model may contribute to the lack of research and policy visibility that reflects the significant problems that some groups face. It is this neglect or 'invisibility' of groups such as the Turks that we seek to challenge.

We are primarily concerned with how the young people in question understand their own situation. The focus is on how the young people deal with economic and cultural obstacles; the role of their communities and families in this transition to adulthood; the impacts of racism and stereotyping; and how the Turkish-speaking groups relate to other young people within their own and in other communities who share similar disadvantages.

In recent discussion of youth transitions, there has been an emphasis on individualisation and risk factors. Roberts (1995, p. 117) argues that:

> In individualized societies it is individuals who have to take the crucial risks with their own lives. They take the decisions and reap the rewards or pay the penalties. It is as if people nowadays embarked on their life journeys without reliable maps, all in private motorcars rather than the trains and buses in which entire classes once travelled together.

In relation to these claims, the aim here is to find out the commonalties of these young people's experiences and structural restrictions in their choices, such as their location in ethnicised labour markets, while at the same time showing how these structural restrictions become more severe in relation to ethnic and gender differences. In addition, we explore whether Kurdish young people are experiencing additional disadvantages because of their refugee status.

This report consists of nine chapters. The first chapter will concentrate on historical and statistical data in relation to the Turkish-speaking community and specifically to young people. Second, we describe our research methodology and characteristics of the sample. The third and fourth chapters consider potential structural barriers, such as families' economic circumstances and the young people's limited educational qualifications, which may impede a more smooth and successful transition to adulthood. The fifth chapter will discuss the young people's actual labour market experiences. The following chapter will concentrate on discrimination and how it may shape the young people's lives. Next, we consider the social side of young people's transitions, namely, how the young people go through their transition to independence, having their own families and households. The penultimate section deals with the young people's transitions in relation to ethnic and religious identity formations. Finally, we will look at how the young people's early experience of adulthood might influence their future aspirations.

1 Turks, Kurds and Turkish Cypriots in Europe: invisible minorities

Patterns of migration

Turkey has a long and complex relationship with the rest of Europe. It is always considered to be 'Other' in Europe, yet it is impossible to comprehend Europe as a whole without referring to Turkey (Triandafyllidou, 2001). Indeed, many Turks, as do Russians, see themselves as part of Europe. A plural society with a significant Christian population, the modern secular Turkish state was founded in the 1920s and has been a bulwark of NATO. Although Turkey has been struggling to join the European Union (EU) for 40 years, it is ironic that the total population of people from Turkey now living in the EU is larger than the population of many EU countries. The EU recently agreed to discuss with Turkey the possibility of it joining the Union, which would give its citizens the right to reside and work in any part of the EU, including Britain. Meanwhile, according to Turkish sources, officially three million (unofficially five million) Turkish people live in various countries in the EU (Uras, 2002). In the 2001 Census in Britain 47,149 individuals stated on their forms that they were of Turkish ethnicity and 13,556 that they were Turkish Cypriots, but many others would simply have ticked options such as 'White Other' without specifying any further details, so no accurate or comprehensive data are available. It has been estimated, however, that there are 80,000 Turkish people living in Britain, of whom 60,000 live in London; in addition, there are estimated to be 120,000 Turkish Cypriots (Onal, 2003). The Turkish community in Europe has a very young population. According to Manco (2001, p. 2), 18 year olds and under constitute a third of the Turkish community in Europe. Eight out of ten of these young people were born and educated in Europe. Moreover, by 2002, there were 82,300 Turkish businesses in the EU, of which 1,600 were in Britain. In the same year, these businesses invested 9.2 billion dollars in the EU and employed 411,000 people (*Milliyet*, 2002). Turks are also to be found in Europe's organised crime. According to Interpol, Turkish gangs have a large share of drug trafficking in Europe (*Avrupa*, 2003). However, a substantial number of Turkish-speaking people in Europe are struggling with economic problems. Regardless of their country of residence, many Turkish-speaking communities are concentrated in deprived neighbourhoods that are ethnically clustered. This is true for the community living in Britain as well. According to the conventional measures of neighbourhood deprivation, in 2000, Haringey was one of the most deprived areas in England (37th out of 354 where 1 is the most deprived) (Neighbourhood Statistics website, http://www.neighbourhoodstatistics.gov.uk/areaProfile). According to the 2001 census, 35 per cent of Haringey's total population of 216,507 come from minority ethnic communities.

Young Turks and Kurds

A Kurdish taxi driver informed us that, in his opinion, North London was not a part of Britain; he felt himself 'in Britain' only when he left North London and visited other places. In North London, he believed that Turkish people have everything they might expect to find in Turkey, apart from some family members. This may not be an exaggeration. In fact, the Turkish-speaking community is probably one of the most self-sufficient communities in London with half a dozen local community-based newspapers, together with Turkish television channels and countless digital radio channels. Community members can provide any service within the community ranging from mortgages to a quit-smoking helpline and from driving instruction to massage parlours. It could be christened 'Little Turkey'.

On the other hand, we cannot talk about a unitary homogeneous community. There are three different groups in the community in Britain, namely Turkish Cypriots, Kurds and mainland Turks. Each of these groups has a different background and set of problems, contrary to the understanding of those outside the community. Since some of these differences are due to their cultural, social and historical backgrounds in Turkey and Cyprus, these differences usually emerge during their interactions with each other. Turkish society in Turkey is not homogeneous and its heterogeneity is reflected in the Turkish-speaking communities throughout Europe, including Britain. In Turkey, there are various ethnic groups, such as Albanians, Georgians, Bosnians, Gypsies, Arabs, Kurds, Bulgarians, Jews and Armenians, but only non-Muslim minorities (namely, Armenians, Jews and Greeks) are regarded as minorities. The other ethnic groups are referred to simply as Turks. However, this does not prevent people from being aware of their differences, especially if they speak a different language in their home. The largest group among these minorities is the Kurds. Since there are no statistical data based on ethnicity in Turkey, it is estimated that there are between ten and 20 million Kurdish people in Turkey.

Kurds are originally from the south-east of the country, but now most of them live in the larger cities in Western Turkey such as Istanbul, Izmir or Ankara, largely because of the internal war between the Turkish army and PKK (Kurdish Workers Party) guerrillas in south-eastern Turkey, which lasted approximately 15 years. The war ended after the capture of the PKK leader, Ocalan, in 1998 and took 35,000 lives, of which 30,000 were Kurdish. During this war, the people were forcibly removed from their villages and ended up in the big cities. Large numbers of people 'disappeared', were tortured and suffered in various ways at the hands of the Turkish special forces, police and army. The war also created a large number of Kurdish refugees, many of whom settled across Europe, including Britain, especially during the peak of the war in the early 1990s. Moreover, most visibly, the Kurdish and Turkish communities in Turkey and in Europe became more nationalistic during the war and this, too, continues to a degree.

The war highlighted the ethnic division between Turks and Kurds, but religious differences too continue to be significant. In Turkey, the majority of people belong to the Sunni sect of Islam, but it is estimated that about 20 per cent belong to a minority sect of Islam, called Alevi, a form of Islam more liberal and sexually egalitarian than many Sunni versions. Those who follow the Alevi faith do not usually go to the mosque and do not pray five times a day. At Ramadan, instead of fasting for 30 days, they fast for only seven. In Turkey, the Alevi and Sunni do not often intermarry and they live in separate villages. There is a history of oppression of the Alevis and, as a consequence, they often do not admit their identity in public. There are Alevis and Sunnis within the different ethnic groups in Turkey. In other words, there are Kurdish Sunnis and Alevis, with their counterparts among Turkish Sunnis and Alevis.

Turkish-speaking groups in Britain

It is inevitable that these historical factors and differences within ethnic group formation have shaped the Turkish-speaking community in Britain. The long street called Green Lane in North London is a snapshot of all of these variations within the community. Turkish Cypriots are an additional variation in Britain, as this group is not present in other European countries. In fact, they were here long before the others, since they had a colonial connection with Britain, unlike other Turkish speakers. They share the Sunni sect with the majority of mainland Turks but do not recognise the variations in religious and ethnic backgrounds in Turkey. To most Turkish Cypriots, anybody from mainland Turkey is simply a Turk.

Turkish-Cypriot males began to migrate to the UK between 1945 and 1955 (Sonyel, 1988, p. 11). Prior to the end of World War II, the majority of the Cypriot population in Britain were of Greek origin; of a total Cypriot population of between 7,000 and 8,000, only 50 were Turkish Cypriots and mostly settled in London (Oakley, 1989, p. 522). According to King and Bridal (1982, p. 95), the fighting between Turkish and Greek Cypriots in Cyprus, which surfaced in the 1950s and intensified in 1963, created pressure on Cypriots to migrate. The bulk of the migration occurred before the worst outbreaks of fighting in 1963–64. The Cypriots chose Britain for their destination because of their colonial link and also because of the high levels of employment in post-war Britain (King and Bridal, 1982, p. 96). Although the census data did not distinguish between Greek and Turkish Cypriots, it is generally agreed that Greeks and Turks left Cyprus at a ratio roughly proportionate to their population on the island, namely four to one (King and Bridal, 1982, p. 97).

The Cypriots are highly concentrated in Greater London. During the main years of Cypriot migration, their number in London increased; however, since 1962, it has fallen slightly. King and Bridal (1982) suggest that an initial settlement in London is customarily followed by dispersal to regional areas on a smaller scale.

Before World War II, early settlers worked in the hotel and restaurant trades, usually in premises owned by Italians. After Italy declared war against Britain, however, most of these Italians went back to their country and Greek Cypriots filled their places in this trade. Oakley (1989) notes that the number of Cypriot cafes and restaurants in London rose from 29 in 1939 to around 200 in 1945.

The other main economic area in which the Cypriot community is concentrated is the textile industry and 'rag trade'. This economic activity was boosted by the arrival of Cypriot women who had traditional village skills of tailoring and dressmaking (King and Bridal, 1982). The initial migration of the young adult males was followed by the women and the gender balance changed from five males to one female in 1931 to parity in 1971. In 1971, half of the employed Cypriot women in Britain worked in the textile and clothing industry.

Furthermore, by utilising female employment, the Cypriot households apparently increased their wealth and this prosperity led to changes in their residential pattern in London (King and Bridal, 1982). In 1951, the Cypriots were concentrated around Camden, Islington and Westminster, and Camden itself became a 'little Cyprus'. By 1961, however, the concentration of the Cypriot population decreased in Westminster, remained constant in Islington and Camden, and increased 20 times in Haringey. By 1966, the Cypriot population in Camden started declining faster than the total borough population (King and Bridal, 1982). Haringey emerged as the second most popular borough for Cypriots, doubling its Cypriot population in the 1961–66 period. The initial location for Cypriots was determined by the location of abundant unskilled employment and the availability of cheap housing. Camden, Westminster and Islington are all near the West End, where London's commercial and entertainment centre is located. It was also an area dominated by the clothing industry after the war. The Cypriots found employment in the hotels, catering and textile industries.

As mentioned earlier, Turkish Cypriots are latecomers compared to their Greek counterparts and, according to Ladbury (1977), they were dependent on the Greek Cypriot community for employment and received assistance for housing. Before 1974, the two communities got along well, but did not socialise outside of work (Ladbury, 1977). In time, Turkish Cypriots also started to have their own businesses and textile factories, and became a self-sufficient community. Moreover, it seems that they followed the same pattern of movement as well. Robins and Aksoy (2001) state that, when Turkish Cypriots first arrived in London, they settled in the Euston and Camden areas, and, when they were able to afford better housing, they moved to Seven Sisters, Haringey, Palmers Green and are now as far out as Enfield.

Turkish migration from mainland Turkey started in the late 1960s and early 1970s with men arriving on their own and bringing their wives and children in the late 1970s and early 1980s (Mehmet Ali, 2001). Although the majority of them came from western parts of Turkey and big cities such as Izmir and Ankara, Mehmet Ali (2001) argues that these migrants originally came from rural areas and migrated first to the big cities in Turkey and later to Britain. Moreover, during the fieldwork, we observed a sizeable community from the Black Sea region. As Turkish Cypriots were initially dependent on Greek Cypriots, similarly, Turkish people probably received support from Turkish Cypriots on arrival. In time, they too started to have their own businesses.

In the late 1980s and early 1990s, Kurdish people arrived in London, mostly as refugees. Again, there is no study showing the historical trend of their movement within London, but, unlike Cypriots and Turks, they seem to have settled down directly in Haringey and Hackney. However, the economic circumstances were not so favourable for them. In this period, the textile industry had become extremely competitive, especially with the influx of cheap products from Eastern European countries. For Kurdish people, saving money in order to own their businesses was therefore more difficult. Yet, like the others, they used their kinship networks to buy their own textile factories, shops or restaurants, usually with their relatives.

The result is that the Turkish, Kurdish and Cypriot communities are working and living in the same areas of London (Mehmet Ali, 2001). However, there are now less favourable economic conditions for all these communities. While there is clearly a Turkish economic enclave, the main industry, textiles, has almost vanished. The main economic unit is shops (such as kebab houses and coffee shops), whose numbers have increased considerably. This makes employment opportunities more restricted and less appealing because of the low wages and long hours characteristic of these shops (Enneli, 2002).

This chapter has pointed to a heterogeneous community, including three groups of migrants with three different historical and social backgrounds, which inevitably have affected relations between the communities in Britain. Our sketch of migration patterns has shown how the groups arrived sequentially and how this affected the life chances of the young people who are the object of our study. Moreover, this sequence of migration has brought to Haringey the recent divisions of Turkish society, especially that between the mainland Turks and the Kurds in the late 1980s and 1990s.

2 Making young Turks and Kurds visible: research methods

The aim of this study was to gather material to begin an exploration of the lives of young Turkish-speaking people and to investigate the specific problems they face in the transition from school to work. A major concern was to allow their distinctive voices to be heard. Thus, our research was small-scale and qualitative. While we did not seek to construct a generalisable and representative sample, we did wish to sketch a broad picture of aspects of these young people's lives that was fairly typical and accurate, against which we could set individual young people's experiences. We began with a questionnaire survey covering our three target groups and tried to include the most vulnerable and disadvantaged young people. The survey then provided us with a base for obtaining a targeted sub-sample for in-depth interviewing.

The London Borough of Haringey was chosen as the site for fieldwork for two reasons. First, it is the main place where Turkish-speaking people are concentrated and where there is some official local recognition and data. We initially wanted to compare some young Bangladeshi people with Turkish-speaking young people. However, we had to abandon this part of the project because of difficulties of access (see Appendix 2). Second, this was the locality for recent work on Turkish schoolchildren, on which this research built (Enneli, 2001).

The survey

Before we started the main fieldwork, we interviewed people from various community organisations. We sought their opinion relating to young people's problems and how to invite young people to participate in our research. In particular, we wanted to know how we could contact the most disadvantaged young people. They suggested we contact various football clubs in the North London area and find young people in these clubs, since football is very popular among the Turkish-speaking people, especially young men. Twenty-one Turkish-speaking football clubs in the area were subsequently contacted. The head of the Turkish-speaking football association introduced us to a female football club and a female volleyball club. In addition, we contacted four community organisations, one college, one employment agency, one youth project supported by the Borough and, finally, three coffee houses.

The methods for collecting data varied between organisations and what they thought would work best for them and their members. More than half of the questionnaires were administered personally by a member of the research team (Enneli) and the rest were returned by post. The college and employment agency asked us to send them individually self-addressed envelopes, which they distributed to a selection of young people. The other organisations asked us to post a set of questionnaires, which they distributed to a selection of young people, and collected once completed and returned to us.

At the end of the survey, we had 250 responses (78 females and 172 males) out of 800 questionnaires circulated. The sample consisted of 99 Turkish, 68 Kurdish, 54 Cypriot and 29 young people of mixed origin. The mixed group consisted of six of Turkish and Kurdish origins, six of Turkish and Cypriot origins, four of Kurdish and Cypriot origins and 13 where only one parent was of Turkish-speaking origins. In terms of age composition of the sample, there were 30 people aged between 16 and 17, 172 aged between 18 and 20 and the rest aged between 21 and 23. We found that the sorting categories we were using (Turk, Kurd, Cypriot, mixed) made sense to our respondents, who were able to self-categorise themselves using these options. Further breakdowns of the survey respondents are given in Tables 1 to 3.

The interviews

One-hundred-and-sixteen respondents agreed to give interviews. We contacted a cross-section of 50 of them to request an interview and achieved our target of 30 interviews (15 males and 15 females). They were chosen to help us further explore certain issues about school and work experiences. We interviewed eight young

Table 1 Characteristics of the sample: gender by ethnicity

	Female (%)	Male (%)	N
Turk	23	77	99
Kurd	25	75	68
Cypriot	41	59	54
Mixed	55	45	29
Total	31	69	250

Table 2 Characteristics of the sample: age distribution by ethnicity

	16–17 (%)	18–20 (%)	21–23 (%)	N
Turk	13	72	15	99
Kurd	16	56	28	68
Cypriot	7	74	19	54
Mixed	7	79	14	29
Total	12	69	19	250

Table 3 Characteristics of the sample: age distribution by gender

	16–17 (%)	18–20 (%)	21–23 (%)	N
Female	10	71	19	78
Male	13	68	19	172
Total	12	69	19	250

Kurds and eight Cypriots (four females and four males in each group), seven Turks (three females and four males) and seven mixed-origin young people (four females and three males).

Twenty-one of the interviews were recorded, with detailed notes taken of the rest, since some young people preferred not to be taped during the interview. The majority of the interviews took one hour to complete. Almost all of the interviews were conducted at Haringey Library, apart from four interviews done at the interviewees' work places and six at the interviewees' homes. Both Turkish and English languages were used during most of the interviews. All the interviews were conducted by Pinar Enneli, a Turkish speaker from mainland Turkey; she translated them into English when necessary.

The interviews were semi-structured, using a topic guide. The topics covered were living conditions; the local environment; their personal history of education, employment, unemployment; family life; identity; religion; and, finally, their future expectations. In Appendix 1, we give some background information for each interviewee with a pseudonym, which we use in order to maintain confidentiality. In addition, we interviewed the parents of six interviewees (two from each group). All of these interviews were recorded.

We presented our draft results to three organisations: Haringey Council, an employment agency and a community organisation that targets Kurdish refugees. We noted their comments on the policy implications of our research. We also sent a one-page summary to 50 young people in order to get their responses. We conducted three focus groups with 12 of these young people (four Kurdish, four Cypriot and four Turkish young people).

In the chapters that follow, we draw on all these data sources to present a picture of young Turkish-speaking origin people's experiences. To make something of their distinct lives visible was a prime aim of our research.

3 A background of disadvantage: Turkish-speaking families' economic circumstances

As described in Chapter 1, migrants from Turkey and northern Cyprus have come to Britain at different times. Therefore, some of the young people in our survey were born in Britain, while others have been here for only a few years. As Table 4 shows, while nearly two-thirds of the young Cypriots were born in Britain, only about a third of the Turks and virtually none of the Kurds were. This clearly affects the economic status and living conditions of not just the young people, but also their families. This also affects the extent of their schooling in Britain and facility in the English language. The differences between earlier and later arrivals are also likely to be coloured by the fact that most of the recent entrants, especially the Kurds, are refugees. As such, they may have fled their homes without many possessions, may not have been able to seek paid employment in Britain for many years and may have suffered displacement and trauma.

Chapter 1 showed how migrants from Turkey and Cyprus established themselves in Britain, moving into distinct economic niches. We described how they were concentrated in certain areas and how certain employment sectors they occupied, such as textiles, had subsequently declined. Thus, our young respondents have grown up against a backdrop of economic deprivation.

As previously mentioned, according to neighbourhood deprivation indices, Haringey is a deprived area. Moreover, the percentage of unemployment in Haringey is 5.8 per cent, compared to the England and Wales average of 3.4 per cent. In addition, three in every ten households in Haringey live in rented social housing (renting from the council, a housing association or a registered social landlord), while less than half of the households own their homes. The remainder of the households rent privately or live rent free (Neighbourhood Statistics website, http://www.neighbourhoodstatistics.gov.uk/areaProfile).

Table 4 Arrival in Britain by ethnicity

	Born in Britain (%)	Before 10 years old (%)	10–15 (%)	After 15 years old (%)	N
Turk	36	24	22	19	97
Kurd	3	43	32	22	68
Cypriot	66	9	15	9	53
Mixed	48	28	14	10	29
Total	35	26	22	17	247

Data missing in three cases.

Turkish-speaking families in Haringey are worse off than the average. Free School Meal (FSM) entitlement for pupils in English schools is an indicator for measuring poverty. In 2002, four out of ten Haringey GCSE cohort students required a free meal, while nearly eight out of ten Kurdish students, 65 per cent of Turkish students and half of the Turkish Cypriot students did so (Haringey Local Education Authority website, http://www.haringey.gov.uk/education/). The Turkish-speaking families in our sample were worse off than the Haringey average in terms of unemployment and home ownership.

Moreover, the differences between Kurdish, Turkish and Cypriot parents are also evident. Kurdish fathers were more likely to be unemployed, compared to Cypriot and Turkish fathers. Besides, no Kurdish fathers had professional jobs, while no Kurdish mothers had their own shops or were in professional employment. As can be seen in Table 5, the unemployment rate is very high among the fathers of our survey respondents. More than half of the young people have an unemployed or retired father, while 21 per cent of them have unskilled or semi-skilled fathers. Eight out of ten mothers are housewives, unemployed or retired, which is quite disproportionate for mothers of teenage children in this country with the exception of Pakistanis and Bangladeshis (Modood *et al.*, 1997). Moreover, more than half of the mothers who are housewives have unemployed husbands. In other words, more than half of the Turkish-speaking households in our survey were without a breadwinner at home. However, there is also a minority of better-off families, which have two parents holding professional jobs or having self-employment.

Table 5 Mother's economic status by father's economic status

Mother's economic status	Father's economic status			
	Unemployed/ retired (%)	Unskilled/ semi-skilled (%)	Self-employed (%)	*N*
Housewife/unemployed/retired	56	22	22	198
Unskilled/semi-skilled jobs	35	21	44	34
Self-employed/professional	28	6	67	18
Total	51	21	28	250

In relation to household ownership, the Turkish-speaking families again are more dependent on social housing than the average for Haringey. As can be seen in Table 6, half of the Turkish-speaking families were living in social rented housing. The number of Kurdish families who were living in social rented housing is even higher (84 per cent). On the other hand, the table shows that 74 per cent of Cypriot families owned their homes, while only 10 per cent of Kurdish families did so. The Turkish and the mixed families are between these two positions.

Table 6 Types of living arrangements by ethnicity

	Social rented housing (%)	Privately rented (%)	Owned (%)	*N*
Turk	49	19	32	98
Kurd	84	6	10	67
Cypriot	17	9	74	53
Mixed	38	24	38	29
Total	50	14	36	247

Data missing in three cases.

As well as these variations between the groups in terms of home-ownership levels, the condition of their houses also varies. For example, during the fieldwork, we observed that the homes of the Cypriots are bigger than those of the Kurds. Household items appeared to be newer and more expensive. The worst off were the Kurdish households that had not yet been granted the right to live permanently in Britain. But even the Kurds who have permanent residence live in smaller houses with much more modest decoration.

The young people are aware of their economic disadvantages, though they might not be familiar with terms such as working class or middle class. Kurdish young people usually think that they are at the bottom of society. For instance, Bengi identified herself as:

> Somebody who is everybody's enemy – bloody refugee and unemployed? I suspect I'm at the bottom somewhere.

As this chapter has indicated, and as we will see elsewhere, the Kurds, as the newest migrant group, suffer the highest levels of disadvantage in their lives, in part linked to the refugee status of many of them; while the longest settled group, the Turkish Cypriots, are the least disadvantaged. This pattern is transmitting itself to the next generation as the following chapters show.

Box 1   Figen: refugee insecurities

Figen, a Kurdish young woman, has been in this country for five years now. These five years were not easy for her and her family. The family's future is uncertain and this creates serious personal and social problems. Figen's parents came to Britain two years earlier than she and her sister, during which time they were left with their grandparents in south-eastern Turkey. After her parents' unsuccessful attempts to bring the family together again, the stress, uncertainty and economic hardship led her mother to attempt suicide.

Continued overleaf

Fortunately, she was rescued and the family then paid a 'company' to smuggle Figen and her sister into Britain by selling all of the remaining possessions in Turkey.

Since then, the family has been struggling to get a positive decision from the Home Office. The Home Office finally rejected their application for asylum on the grounds that the family went to Germany first and wanted to send them back to Germany. The family is terrified of this prospect, as Figen believes that the German authorities will send them back to Turkey within a week; and, without passports, all of them could be kept in prison for at least a week for interrogation. All members of the family are fixed on one thing, that is not going back to Turkey.

Economically, life here is not that comfortable, as her parents are unemployed. And, because they are not guaranteed asylum, the local authorities provide them with only temporary accommodation and refuse to add them to the housing list. In these five years, the family have moved four times. Their only possession, apart from their clothes, is a carpet bought by a relative as a present. Both Figen and her sister give 'help' to some relatives in their shops. She feels as if everybody in this country is trying to get rid of them because they are refugees. Figen has experienced discrimination in school and she believed that:

> They always pick on the one who is silent and the one who tries to concentrate on study. So the best way is to get along with them, not answering back and not showing off when the teacher asked something in the class.

However, she still prefers to be here rather than in Turkey, believing that she has 'more chances here, both economic and education opportunities'. University would be an option if she could sort out her language problem and also if the family were given the right to remain in this country.

Figen does not feel British, but would like to have citizenship in this country for security reasons. She calls herself Kurdish and/or Alevi and has a boyfriend who is Kurdish. While she believes that her family would respect her choice of partner, if she decides to marry, she would still prefer somebody Kurdish and Alevi.

4 Struggling to learn: education and qualifications

Our aim in this research is to analyse the fragmented and unpredictable nature of young people's transitions to adulthood. Accordingly, we asked them about their experiences during and after compulsory schooling. It is obvious that their school experiences and qualifications affected their chances in the labour market, yet we were less interested in their position at the time of the interview, but, rather, in the whole experience of transition to adulthood. In this respect, this chapter considers Turkish-speaking young people's views on their school experience and how it may have affected their labour market chances.

From the perspective of our respondents, their school experience is generally not a good one. The school often appears to them as an alienating environment. One result of this is that many of the 16–23 year olds who filled in our questionnaire did not have many qualifications. This outcome is also likely to be shaped by their socio-economic background and, in the case of some, their recent arrival under difficult circumstances in Britain.

Nearly half of the males and 37 per cent of the females in our survey did not have a single good GCSE result. In terms of the 2002 GCSE results, only 13 per cent of 99 Kurdish candidates achieved five or more C and above grades (the standard measure of good educational achievement). For Turkish Cypriots, it was 14 per cent of 36 and, for Turkish students, 21 per cent of 94. The average for Haringey is 35 per cent (Haringey Local Education Authority website, http://www.haringey.gov.uk/education/).

This distribution of qualifications is clearly related to the period of years in Britain, as is shown in Table 7. More than four out of ten of those who have no GCSEs arrived in Britain over the age of 15; the longer someone had been in Britain, the higher their qualification.

Table 7 Being born in Britain by qualification

	Born in Britain (%)	Before 10 years old (%)	10–15 (%)	After 15 years old (%)	N
None	5	14	38	43	95
Only GCSEs	61	35	4	–	23
Only GNVQ	29	42	29	–	45
Only A levels	78	14	8	–	49
Both GNVQ and A levels	46	51	3	–	35
Total	35	26	22	17	247

Data missing in three cases.

If students do reach GCSEs, they invariably go on to achieve some additional qualifications, as is shown in Table 8. The table makes clear that the problem is not so much that the Turkish-speaking young people are uniformly at the bottom end of qualifications, rather that, as a group, they have a bipolar distribution. Four out of ten Turks have no qualifications; but more than half have at least one A level or one GNVQ. Similarly, nearly six out of ten Kurds are without any qualifications but 37 per cent have a qualification higher than a GCSE (Table 8). In other words, very few stop at GCSE; either they do not get there, or they go beyond it. This is also the experience of Pakistanis and Bangladeshis, though most other groups are less bipolar (Modood *et al.*, 1997; Modood, 2003).

It is sometimes suggested – or hoped – that vocational qualifications might play a major role for those not interested in an academic pathway. In our interviews, however, we found that GNVQs are not working as an alternative career path. The young people usually took GNVQ courses because they could not take any A levels. Some of the young people did these courses without a particular aim in mind, like Hasan, a young Kurd:

When I was in the secondary school, the only thing in my mind is to finish the school and start working. Then, a couple of months after the school, I couldn't find a job. Then my mother told me either work or go to college. I chose college. I'm doing basic GNVQ in mechanical engineering.

Most of the Turkish-speaking young people did not have many qualifications to help them in the labour market. One of the reasons regarding the lack of qualifications was that most of the respondents attended what they themselves considered to be 'sink schools'. This was particularly true of schools in Haringey, to which the Kurds were more than twice as likely to have gone. Ceylan, a Kurdish female described her school:

Nobody expect us do well especially in the exams ... because you're in this bad school, you should be bad as well ... It's like you're a loser in a loser school.

Table 8 Qualifications by ethnicity

	None (%)	Only GCSEs (%)	GNVQ (%)	A level (%)	Both GNVQ and A level (%)	*N*
Turk	40	8	19	20	12	99
Kurd	57	6	15	10	12	68
Cypriot	24	7	22	26	20	54
Mixed	21	24	14	28	14	29
Total	39	9	18	20	14	250

The Turkish-speaking young people did not seem to have received enough support from the staff in the school in order to tackle their problems, including educational achievement. Ogun, a young Turkish man, explained his frustration towards the teachers:

Teachers, like police, always came late … They only came when they hear very loud screams.

Furthermore, the Turkish-speaking young people, especially the Kurds, have language difficulties. As Leyla argued:

I believe I could do better in the exams, if my English was not like this. You know, during the exams, they told us that no dictionaries were permitted.

Moreover, regardless of the area the Turkish-speaking young people came from, the schools they went to were made up almost entirely of minority ethnic pupils. There seemed to be a great deal of tension between different groups, which sometimes ended with physical fighting. Sinem, a Turkish girl, shared her experiences with us:

In the school, one friend of mine was stabbed. He was hit on his face with a glass, then stabbed with a broken glass … *[The male was black and the stabbed friend was Turkish]*.

Those without qualifications were more likely to be caught up in these ethnic tensions, but, in general, all young people, especially young men, tended to have their own groups in schools. The groups were often based on ethnicity, but were sometimes mixed. Being a member of such a group brought its own rules and created enemies. Nazim, a young Turkish man who stated that his best experience in school was the leaving day, because he didn't need to go back there ever again:

In my school, there were three groups, predominantly black. I tried to be a part of a middle group, which is not that powerful, but not weak either.

These factors are likely to contribute to the young people's under-achievement in exams and high levels of truancy and exclusions. About a third of the young people from each ethnic group had played truant during their education. It was mainly the boys who did so. Almost half the males in the survey said that they truanted when they were in school, while the number of females who truanted was much less (15 per cent).

When some individuals were not able to solve their problems, they stopped attending school, or they got involved in various fights, some of which were quite serious. In the end, they gave up on school altogether. For instance, Firat, a Kurdish male, wanted to be a computer engineer and ended up working in a grocery shop owned by his family. He explained what had gone wrong in his education:

The school became more and more boring. First I started with small truancies. Just one class I didn't like at all. Then I didn't go to school for a whole day, then a couple of days … In the final year, I just wanted to get over it and start working.

Apart from truancy, exclusion was also a considerable problem for the Turkish-speaking young people, especially the Kurds, nearly a quarter of whom had been excluded (Table 9).

The main reason for this is that the young people are constantly involved in ethnic tensions and physical fights. Firat explains why he was excluded from the school:

I had a fight with one of the English guys. I don't remember exactly why. It's not important stuff, just he said something nasty and I said something back and I beat him.

These young people did not have positive school experiences and were not academically successful, nor were they well prepared for the labour market. On the other hand, especially in recent years, alternative employment scenarios have become available to these young people through the gang culture. Firat spoke at length about gangs:

Some of them are well known like Bombs. And couple of others. These are known. There are more unknown groups. There are young people who try to own their own gangs. They pretend *[to be]* these famous ones. I don't know listening to different music, going around with friends, beating up others. I mean they get money by beating people … There is this idea called 'bad boy'. For

Table 9 Exclusion by ethnicity

	Yes (%)	No (%)	*N*
Turk	16	84	101
Kurd	24	76	66
Cypriot	13	87	52
Mixed	21	79	29
Total	18	82	248

instance, you should be very hard. I mean, I am a 'bad boy' I can beat you. Then he *[another boy]* will beat me and we together can beat him. It's go on and on. That's the attitude … There are some groups in the schools. I mean the number of groups involving clever student is only two or three, but that of not clever ones are 200 or 300.

Another Kurdish male, Hasan, asked me to stop recording when I asked him his suggestions on what could be done to improve young people's conditions in the area:[1]

They should do something about the mafia. Because several mafia support various gangs here. Not only Turkish or Kurdish, but Irish, black. They all have their own gang groups. They all passed their dirty jobs to the gang. They buy nice cars for these boys and give some money as well.

A Cypriot female, Jale, also shared her observations about gang culture with us:

The Turkish people I see apart from my friends … either went onto drugs or they're rough or they're driving around in their cars thinking they're bovver boys and things like that.

In grappling with their problems at school, the Turkish young people were able to get only limited help from their parents, although many tried to do their best to support their children. The six parents who were interviewed appeared to have little idea of the young people's problems in school. All of them said that they were involved in their children's education, attended parents' evenings and saw the teachers regularly. Yet, almost all of the parents admitted that, before their children went to school, they did not know much about the system but they learnt more over the years. Moreover, all of them thought that their children's school, including the teachers, was one of the best. Although they were generally aware of their children's educational problems, they did not question the school system and instead accused the families themselves of not giving the right values to their children.

Recent research into the youth labour market (for example, Furlong and Cartmel, 1997; Fenton *et al.*, 2001; Jones, 2002) has highlighted the crucial role of education in setting young people onto a 'winning' path in life. Qualifications are an important form of human capital, which equips people for job and career success. Research has long shown that educational progress is dependent on families (Bates and Riseborough, 1993); more advantaged parents can help with homework, negotiate with teachers and steer their children through the school system. The Turkish-speaking families for the most part cannot provide such support, and, thus, the young Turks and Kurds must fend for themselves in a school system that is particularly rife with ethnic conflicts and apparent teacher disinterest in their special problems.

These young people, then, did not display much motivation and engagement with their schooling. A destructive peer culture based on ethnically differentiated gangs seemed to be at the core of this, with ethnic conflicts, racism and bullying deterring young Turkish-speaking people from studying. Teachers in such disadvantaged and ethnically torn schools may have an uphill struggle to perform effectively, but there was no evidence in our interviews of any encouragement or help from teachers. The perception of some of our respondents was that allowances are made for other groups at the expense of the Turks. This was the perception of Ayca, who was excluded for getting into a fight with a black student:

> The teacher saw us. I got excluded. The other girl didn't. I don't know why … They told 'it doesn't matter who started the fight. You were in a fight. So you're gonna be excluded' … She should get excluded. But they didn't listen to me … because she is a black student. They don't wanna do it to her … Though she was in the fight as well, they would like to make excuses for her. Because she had been in lots of fights before, it was like, if she was in one more fight, that's it, then she's out of school. And they made excuses for her.

It may be that, more generally, teachers are more able to 'see' the problems of 'visible minorities' such as the African Caribbeans, and that the invisibility of the Turks means that their particular problems are not noticed or grasped by teaching staff. Much schooling is subsequently missed through truancy and exclusions. Concerned parents are not able to help because of language difficulties and their limited understanding of the educational system. Many of the young Turkish-speakers thus end their schooling demotivated, uninterested and without qualifications.

5 Risky transitions: entering the labour market

As stated in the introduction, transitions from school to work are becoming more risky, fragmented and extended for all young people. The family backgrounds and educational disadvantage discussed suggest that the risks are heightened for these young Turkish-speaking people. In relation to these claims, the aim here is to find out about the commonalties of these young people's experiences and structural restrictions on their choices – such as their confinement to ethnic economies. In this chapter, we will discuss the unemployment and employment experiences of the young people.

In recent years, there has been particular concern in Britain directed at young people who leave full-time education at the minimum age of 16 and then spend a substantial period not in education, employment, or training (NEET) (e.g. Bynner and Parsons, 2002). As mentioned in the introduction, many of the young people from ethnic minorities are particularly hard to access as they are disproportionately represented among the Government's NEET category. We were fortunate in finding and including in our survey young unemployed people who have not had a job or any training.

In our survey, 60 per cent of those who had been unemployed at some time had not received any sort of training, including in-work training, language or computer courses. Moreover, 25 per cent of the unemployed had never had a job.

Yet, it has to be said, this does not tell the full story. For, during the interviews, we realised that the young people's engagement in the labour market is more complex than simply being in and out of jobs or attending a course. The following two sections analyse these complexities.

Unemployment

The young people were asked if they had ever been unemployed since leaving school. It is important to stress that this is a self-defined measure of unemployment, not an 'official' measure of registered unemployment. This reflects our desire to see their world as much as possible through their eyes. The experience of unemployment is usually dependent on young people's age, gender, ethnicity, qualifications and their families' economic conditions, factors which were also used in our analysis of employment status.

It seems that those younger than 18 were least likely to experience unemployment (23 per cent), while over a third of those over 18 had been unemployed (Table 10). Of course, this is partly a factor of time: the older someone is, the less likely they are to be in education or training; and those who have been longer out of education and training are more likely to have had a spell of unemployment. However, during the interviews, we found that, in general, the young people without regular work sometimes did not call themselves unemployed unless they were actively looking for a job. During this time, they may have taken on some irregular work, but they described this in terms of doing a favour for somebody they knew. However, this would not necessarily be seen as 'employment'; and possibly not as 'unemployment' either. The point is that 'unemployment' consists of looking for and not having regular paid work on a formal basis. Periods of irregular work are not seen as 'unemployment' but are not considered 'proper employment' either. They call it 'helping' somebody they know for a short period. For instance, we interviewed Bengi, a Kurdish female, in a coffee shop where she was helping for a couple of weeks, but she said she did not have a job. She said:

> I'm not working really. I'm just helping him since he is a very close relative and he couldn't find somebody else ... I mean, I can't call myself a working person.

Aysegul, a girl of mixed origin, postponed her interview three times because of last-minute requests from a friend or family member for help in their shops, and yet she too was 'unemployed'.

Males were more likely to have been unemployed than females. Thirty-six per cent of the males had experienced unemployment since leaving school, compared to 28 per cent of females. The males were also both more likely to be unemployed more than once and unemployed in the first year after school.

For example, Baris, a Cypriot, explained the difficulties of being unemployed:

> Getting money off my parents, it's not good. I don't feel right. I like to work ... you can't spend money when you want ... when you go to college, to buy food and you can't eat nothing and things like that.

Table 10 Ever unemployed since leaving school by age

	Yes (%)	No (%)	N
16–17	23	77	30
18–20	35	65	172
21–23	33	67	48
Total	34	66	250

The difficulties were not just financial. Ebru, a young Cypriot woman, recalls her period of unemployment as consisting of endless TV and going shopping with her mother, and not a time of doing what you pleased:

If I was asked like … 'how are you?'. 'Oh, I'm bored'. And they go, 'don't be silly. You don't have to wake up, you don't have to do anything.' Well, they've got the wrong idea of being unemployed!

In terms of ethnicity, there was a clear ranking of ethnic groups in relation to unemployment. As Table 11 indicates, the Kurds and Turks were less likely to experience unemployment, while the Cypriots were the most likely. This is somewhat paradoxical, as the Cypriots were, by other measures, the best off. It may be that the Kurds and Turks were not actively looking for work and so, as our interviews suggest, did not count themselves as unemployed; some people's refugee status may not have allowed them to work; or it may be that they could not afford to be unemployed and were ready to accept any job that they could find. As Leyla said:

It's like the job chose you, instead of you chose the job. There are lots of off-licences, coffee shops or kebab shops opening in this area every week. And they always need somebody.

Unemployment, then, may depend more on the family being able to afford it or not, rather than having difficulties in finding a job. Alpay, a Cypriot, is a typical example. His father owns a dry-cleaning shop and asked Alpay to work for him after school. But Alpay said that he did not want to and wanted to take some time out. As a result, his family stopped giving him money and, in his words, he 'had to work to get it at his father's shop'. It is probably, however, the Kurds who can least afford to be unemployed and seem to enter or seek to enter the labour market as early as they can.

Table 11 Ever unemployed since leaving school by ethnicity

	Yes (%)	No (%)	*N*
Turk	31	68	99
Kurd	29	48	68
Cypriot	41	32	54
Mixed	38	18	29
Total	34	66	250

This is consistent with the findings of Table 12, which show that young people with GCSEs were more likely to experience unemployment than those with no qualifications (though those with A-level qualifications were least likely to have experienced unemployment). Again, we stress that 'unemployment' cannot be taken at its face value, in the light of our finding in the interviews that there was a tendency for the young people to not call themselves unemployed unless they were looking for a job. Equally interesting was that they would call themselves 'unemployed' even if they were seeking only part-time work. For example, some with GCSE qualifications who were continuing in education nevertheless called themselves unemployed because they were looking for part-time work. They saw no contradiction in describing themselves as in study and unemployed at the same time.

This need for part-time work, and hence its absence as 'unemployment', arises from the fact that many young people need to make a financial contribution to their living expenses while in education, and even to some of the costs associated with education. Duygu, a Turkish girl, worked during her college education, but, for two months, she was unemployed and states that:

> When you are studying, this is a very long gap, because you have to spend some money for the school. I mean for books and clothes. And also, when we went to trips, I spend my own money. My father only gave money for commuting to the school.

In fact, we found that, regardless of the families' economic conditions, the young people were often expected to pay at least some of the cost of their education through work. For instance, we interviewed two Cypriot young women in their homes. They were each living in a newly decorated, four-bedroom house. Both women were doing their A levels and expecting to go to university. They had been working through their college education to pay for their travel costs, lunch and books. Both of them thought that this was a 'natural' way of continuing their education, because it was 'their responsibility'. They both wanted to go to a university in London. During lunch with Ebru's family, her mother talked about how important it was for them to send her to university and we started to talk about the University of Bristol, and the cost of being a student there. Having been told that it might cost

Table 12 Young people's qualifications by ever unemployed since leaving school

	Yes (%)	No (%)	N
No qualifications	34	66	109
Only GCSE level	45	55	56
GCSE and A level	26	74	85
Total	34	66	250

about £500 per month, she made a quick calculation in her mind and said 'Oh God! It is that much. I don't think we can afford it.' Whether going to a local university (and perhaps having to live at home for financial reasons) or further afield, most of these young people would need to be in regular part-time employment in order to afford higher education.

During the interviews with the families, there was general agreement that young people should make a financial contribution to the cost of their post-16 education. On the other hand, there were differences between relatively well-off families and poor ones. The relatively well-off families spoke of this issue in moral terms, justifying it as teaching the young people responsibility and the facts of life. For the young people from poor families, paid work is often a necessity if they are to continue their education. For instance, a refugee mother said that, although she appreciated the importance of education for her children's future, she could see no way of providing financial support for them, since she and her husband were unemployed and living in temporary accommodation.

The young people's understanding of unemployment, then, is more complex than simply being out of work. Some of them did not call themselves unemployed although they were not in regular work. On the other hand, some called themselves unemployed while in further education, as they often needed a part-time job to fund their continuing education and, thus, were actively seeking work. This does mean that 'unemployed' is a confusing term and there is considerable ambiguity about the exact employment status of the people in the study. As explained, however, we did not define 'employed' and 'unemployed' in our questionnaires but let the young people interpret the terms in their own way.

Allowing, then, that 'unemployed', for at least some of our respondents, relates to active search for a job (including a part-time job), regardless of whether one is officially unemployed, in education or receiving training, it nevertheless seems that there is a further distinction in the two types of unemployment experienced by the Turkish-speaking young people. One type of unemployment is experienced by highly excluded young people from economically disadvantaged families, with few or no qualifications. The other type of unemployment is experienced by relatively well-off young people, who have family support during unemployment and can afford to be selective in the labour market, or who may be between periods of study or even in study. Furthermore, there are clear gender and ethnic differences in terms of unemployment. In general, males and Kurdish young people are more likely to be in the first category of unemployment.

Bearing in mind all the complexities of Turkish-speaking young people's experience of unemployment and their perceptions of employment, the next section will focus on employment experiences of these young people in detail. The discussion will focus on the nature of the jobs held by these young people.

Employment

The young people's understanding of paid employment complements how they understood unemployment. Almost 35 per cent of males and 44 per cent of females said that they have had no paid employment since leaving school. These figures are higher than for those who said they have ever been unemployed. It seems that, just as some respondents may not have called themselves unemployed, unless they were looking for a job, similarly, some may not have referred to their job as 'paid employment', unless it was regular, external (non-familial) employment.

It can thus be seen that, although the females are less likely to experience unemployment, they are also less likely to be working. In other words, it seems that some of the young women were not actively seeking employment and stayed out of the labour market. For instance, Sinem, a Turkish female, had three A levels. In 2000, and before going to university, she decided to have some time for herself without studies; during this period, she worked in a couple of jobs but on the whole she 'didn't do anything':

> I wanted to have a break first. I don't know, I didn't think so much about it. I mean, after my A levels, it seemed reasonable to have a one-year gap. Then one year became two years. I don't know.

In relation to ethnicity, as Table 13 indicates, the Kurdish young people are less likely to say they have had paid employment since they left school. Yet, we found, during the interviews, they were in fact sometimes working. However, in those situations, they tended to view it as 'helping somebody'. Hasan, who was only able to manage to meet for an interview at seven o'clock at night after work, said:

> I don't work. I'm just filling a friend's place. He went on holiday to Turkey for three weeks.

On the other hand, young people's qualifications and their families' economic backgrounds also affect whether they have paid employment. Almost 70 per cent of the young people with unemployed or retired fathers have had paid employment since leaving school. Bearing in mind that mothers who are housewives are more likely to have unemployed husbands, the young people's employment therefore can be important for the household. Leyla, whose mother and father are both

Table 13 Ever in paid employment since leaving school by ethnicity

	Yes (%)	No (%)	*N*
Turk	60	40	97
Kurd	53	47	68
Cypriot	78	22	54
Mixed	66	34	29
Total	63	38	248

Data missing in two cases.

unemployed, was working in a coffee shop five days a week from 9.00 to 6.00 and earned £130 a week. Although she did not give all of her pay to her family, she still bought food, and from time to time clothes, for her family.

The young people with self-employed parents, on the other hand, helped out in their family's businesses, usually a shop. This was often their main source of income during their education, or in those early years of transition. This is not just in relation to one's parents' businesses but in the family more broadly. Doruk, a Cypriot male at university and living away from his family, explains:

> I'm currently working for my cousin in a shop … The money I earn there pays my rent and my student loans help support my other financial needs.

In general, it seems that quite a number of them managed to find some kind of (part-time) employment within the Turkish-speaking economic enclave or through the community network. This work is usually unskilled or semi-skilled. Even the young people with more than five good GCSE results are willing to work in unskilled jobs. This might be because they do not think of their first job as being permanent. Sinem worked as a receptionist in a dentist's practice, as an office worker in a local newspaper and finally acquired another office job; she was not interested in finding better jobs despite her three A levels:

> When I went to work, it wasn't the work. Because I always thought I've got to go back to studying, which was my plan. That's why I didn't wanna settle into a job … when I was working in the newspaper or others, they were just pass the time jobs. You know, just passing time.

Table 14 demonstrates that the young people with A levels are least likely to work in full-time jobs. In other words, although most of the young people are working in unskilled jobs, the engagement of the young people with A levels in these jobs is quite different. It is seen as a temporary, part-time phase to support their studies and allow them to apply for entirely different kinds of jobs.

Table 14 Qualifications by type of employment

	Full-time (%)	Part-time (%)	N
None	67	33	55
Only GCSEs	64	38	14
Only GNVQ	55	45	31
Only A levels	44	56	25
Both GNVQ and A levels	52	48	23
Total	58	42	148

Working conditions are more difficult for Kurdish young people, especially refugees, since they are the least qualified and most disadvantaged. Although Avni, a Turkish male, is not a refugee because of his British wife, in the first year of his arrival, he worked in a kebab shop. He described the conditions there:

> Every newcomer has to work in a kebab shop once. There is no escape from this. Believe me or not, I worked 84 hours a week and only earned £115.

Furthermore, almost all of the young people found employment through their relatives and friends. Few used formal job-search methods such as Job Centres. A couple of young Cypriots and Turks actually applied to a Job Centre for help, but none of them was satisfied with the service they received. Sinem said:

> It's so mechanised you know. It's not personal. You just go to there and look at the computer screen, if any available jobs match with your qualifications. And, if there isn't any, there is no chance for you to see somebody and talk about yourself. It's useless really.

On the other hand, most of the negative employment conditions were attributed to the Turkish-speaking employers. They were less valued compared to other employers. Avni said:

> I prefer to work for an English employer, because then you know how much money you get and how long you work. I mean, after 5.00, you can leave the job, whatever you do. But, with a Turkish employer, he says 'go on, let's finish this'. Then you realise, the time is eight o'clock in the evening.

In this chapter, it has been shown that the young people's early experiences in the labour market were affected by age, gender and ethnicity. It is clear that some of these young people, who were often simultaneously studying and working, or happy to be temporarily drifting, did not identify themselves as being simply unemployed, or being in paid employment. Moreover, they did not necessarily feel that they would settle down in the jobs they were doing at the time. Some of the young people with qualifications did not feel that they were rewarded for them in terms of employment. And almost all the young people rely on their community networks in order to find employment.

It seems that these patterns of labour market behaviour are in part voluntary and are heavily influenced by the resources and practices of families and communities. The young Turks, Kurds and Turkish Cypriots clearly use, indeed rely on, family and kin links to help them through risky and extended transitions. There is definitely an ethnic enclave present, consisting of not just sandwich and kebab shops but also other family businesses providing extensive services. In many ways, this is operating as a parallel micro-economy and is clearly a resource that is not available to all disadvantaged groups. However, it has to be stressed that this resource comes at a price. Its existence may be a contributing factor to the young people's relative reluctance to engage with the broader structure of labour market opportunities and can lead to them being trapped in an ethnic enclave.

Transition to independent lives does not only mean labour market inclusion. Transition to adulthood also includes having independent households, or having a family. Therefore, we must also consider this dimension of transition. Before doing so, however, we will briefly discuss the issue of racism and discrimination.

Box 2   Nazim: failing schools or failing pupils?

Nazim was born in this country and has spent all his life in North London; he has no qualifications. He originally wanted to be a police officer, but he finished school with no GCSEs after a very bad school experience, which included truancy and exclusion. Nazim has been unemployed and has tried several jobs, usually in retail. His family was originally from the Black Sea region in Turkey. His father came to this country in the 1960s. After a couple of years, he went to Turkey and married his neighbour's daughter in the village; the couple then came to Britain. He and his wife worked in textile factories. After a while, he owned a textile factory, then a kebab shop and now he is retired. He can write and read Turkish and a little bit of English, but his wife is illiterate.

Nazim has one sister and one brother, both born in this country. He started to play truant in Year 7. During his secondary school education, he was a regular truant and he was also excluded three times from school. On one occasion, he beat up an 'English guy' who called him a 'fucking Turk'. Nazim said that his best experience at school was the last day, because he didn't need to go back there ever again, having found the school environment hostile and full of

Continued overleaf

discrimination. No help was given by his teachers he believed, for they were concerned only with punishment. His mother wanted him to be successful in school, but, according to Nazim, she could not understand the problems he faced and he did not want her to become more sad and frustrated about his future. Nazim has a distant relationship with his father and thinks that only his brother understands his problems, since he himself had attended the same school.

Nazim did not look for a job immediately after school. Instead, he spent a couple of months with his friends drinking in pubs, driving in friends' cars and chasing girls. After a while, his father said 'enough is enough' and forced him either to work in the kebab shop he owned or find another job. Nazim said that he did not resent this ultimatum as he was bored of doing nothing anyway. He left his CV at shops around Wood Green Shopping Centre but heard nothing from them. With the help of his friend, he worked in a couple of shops around the area. Finally, he found a job in a sports shop also with a friend's help.

In his last job, he was promoted to shop manager and believed that he deserved it, as he worked very hard. However, he said that his wages did not match the position he had achieved and, thus, he complained about it. His employer's response was that he was too young to be paid more. Nazim believes that it is not his age but the fact that he is Turkish that is the problem, since his area manager is not much older than him.

Nazim said that when he manages to get a very good job, a beautiful wife, together with a beautiful house, he will feel successful. He believes that he can achieve this aim, though he is realistic. He said:

> For the future, my only advantage is my current job, because I didn't get anything from school. I mean I don't have any GCSE, no college, nothing. I have only my employment experiences in this job. I mean I am working as a shop manager in this shop now. Other than this, I have no advantages.

6 'Why don't you go back home!': discrimination and harassment

We have seen that the young people in this study suffered disadvantage at school and in the labour market. Is this merely because of their economic and class location, or is it also a result of racist discrimination? Do the young people themselves feel that they are victims of racism?

It is well known that non-white ethnic minorities experience discrimination and harassment at school, in the labour market, in employment and in other areas of society (Modood *et al.*, 1997). There is also some evidence that this is also the case today for at least one white group, namely the Irish (Hickman and Walter, 1997), not to mention vestiges of the historic exclusion of Jews. The extent of the contemporary discrimination and racial abuse against white groups may not be the same as against non-whites (which, too, of course may vary between groups and between different spheres of society; see CMEB, 2000, Chapter 5). The evidence from our research suggests that some young Turkish-speaking people believed that they experience discrimination and harassment from white people and some minority groups, and also from other Turkish-speaking groups.

We asked the young people if they had ever been discriminated against for reasons to do with their race or colour, or their religious or cultural background. The question was deliberately broad, for we were not just asking about discrimination in formal situations, such as job applications. We wanted to cover any kind of unfavourable or unpleasant treatment connected to their perceived ethnic background. Nevertheless, we used the term 'discrimination' in our question, since, while it is not entirely accurate, we thought that the alternative terms such as 'racism' or 'ethnicism' were even more susceptible to misunderstanding.

Table 15 shows that a third of the young people in the survey said that they experienced discrimination. There is not much variance between different groups, though Kurdish young people are slightly more likely to experience discrimination (38 per cent). This may not appear a very high level of self-reported discrimination, but this is a topic where people may not like to admit what they have experienced in order to 'save face'. In fact, the interviews strongly highlighted racism and racial tensions.

Table 15 Experiencing discrimination by ethnicity

	Yes (%)	No (%)	N
Turk	27	73	99
Kurd	38	62	68
Cypriot	37	63	54
Mixed	34	66	29
Total	33	67	250

Young Turks and Kurds

Discrimination is a complex and multidirectional phenomenon. Each group has experienced discrimination or disrespect in different ways and for different reasons. Many young people have experienced discrimination by white people, like Ebru's feeling of being judged against a stereotype:

> In the school, I heard one teacher talk to another about me. She said 'this Turkish girl Ebru, she is surprisingly intelligent, isn't she'. Obviously, she doesn't expect me to be intelligent.

Moreover, they experience harassment from people from other ethnic minorities. Some of these are just bad name calling or shouting, such as Duygu's experience:

> The blacks make jokes about your clothes. Because, you know, they like the labels. If you do not wear the label, then they pick on you.

Huseyin had been taunted for another reason:

> When I was in the school, my English was not so good. There were Pakistani children in the class. They always made jokes about my English. Whatever I said they made jokes. It's not good.

Some of the Cypriot and Turkish young people also experienced discrimination from Greek Cypriots. Cahide said:

> They're always … saying 'Cyprus is, you know – Cyprus before and they took it away from us and we don't like Turkish people because of that'.

Sometimes these tensions might involve physical fights, as in the case of Ayca, a Turkish female. Ayca, as mentioned in Chapter 4, was involved in a physical fight with a black student, which resulted in her being excluded for a week. Moreover, the young Turkish speakers also victimise each other. The Kurds are most often picked on, mainly because of the internal war in Turkey and their assertion of a separate identity. Nazim, a Turkish male argued that:

> If we beat a black boy on the street and if he shouts 'they beat me because I am black', every black person on the street comes to help him. But if a Turkish boy is beaten and if he shouts they beat me because I am Turkish, and if a Kurdish person passed by, he joins the attackers and beats the Turkish boy. Of course the opposite is true as well.

Hasan talked about the fight between Kurdish and Turkish people after a football match, when Turkey played in the 2002 World Cup:

> You know the guy who was beaten after the match. He is not even Kurdish. And he is a very old man. He put up his hand like this *[victory sign]* and the others thought he is Kurdish.

Kurdish people are also discriminated against because of their refugee status. Leyla talked about her experience:

> Sometimes other girls say to me: 'Why are you here? Go back to your country.' And, in the council, the officer told me we are taking resources from the people in this country.

Because of these experiences, some of the young refugees hide their status and lie about it, as Huseyin explained:

> I didn't tell the girls that I am refugee, because they don't like refugees. I told them I have a British passport.

Alevis, a religious group within the minority sect of Islam, the Shia, are discriminated against by the Sunni majority in Turkey and this has carried over to London. Leyla talked about her neighbour:

> We have a neighbour. They are Turkish and they know we are Kurdish. But we were good neighbours until they learned that we are Alevi. They stopped their visits immediately; you know that thing that you can't even drink a glass of water from the hands of an Alevi. Rubbish, but some people are like that.

Young mixed-origin people are a vulnerable group who experience discrimination because they are both Kurdish and Turkish. They choose to ignore or switch identities. Murat, an Alevi whose father is Kurdish and mother is Turkish, said:

> Here I said I am Turkish on occasions and I am Kurdish on other occasions. I can be anybody. But you know, in this country, it is not important who you are, the important thing is what is your ability. Anyway, they think I am Turkish, because of my appearance, they think I'm from Izmir or Black Sea. You know one of the Izmir boys with green eyes. Anyway, it's easier to say I am Kurdish in this country. If you dare, go to Turkey and say I'm Kurdish!

The Kurds may be the most oppressed group in Turkey, but some expressed the view that, in London, they are more assertive. This is how Kaya put it:

Of course I am different. I am not totally Turkish, or Kurdish. Do I want to be? I don't know. Maybe life will be easier, but then now I can access all sides of the story. For instance, the Kurdish people said they are discriminated. But, if a boy had a necklace with Ali's sword on it, nobody insults him. But, if they see a boy with Turkish flag necklace, they will beat him. There are so many Kurdish people coming from Turkey to give concerts here. Nothing happens. But, if a Turkish person comes here for a concert, Kurdish people come and interrupt the concert. It happened before.

Females and males experience discrimination differently. As can be seen in Table 16, the males are less likely to state they have experienced discrimination.

This may be because women also experience sexual discrimination and so are more aware of discrimination. It may not necessarily mean that males experience less discrimination. During the interviews, it emerged that some men may find it hard to admit to discrimination, thinking that to do so makes them somehow less masculine. As Alpay, a Cypriot, explained:

In our school, people say things racially a lot ... black this, black that. Turkish this, Turkish that, yes. Well, they didn't really say it to us much because no one had the guts to if you know what I mean ... because we had the reputation and no one would have said it to us. But the black people got it a lot.

Young men may counter racism with bravado and group solidarity, but this strategy is more difficult for females to adopt.

Table 16 Experiences of ethnic discrimination by gender

	Yes (%)	No (%)	N
Female	38	62	78
Male	31	69	172
Total	33	67	250

Our research reveals a complex and disturbing situation. The main site for young people's experience of 'discrimination' – of the negative treatment of 'difference' – seems to be the school. Here, there is some evidence of what the McPherson Report (1999) has called institutional racism, namely, inferior treatment of persons because of unconscious assumptions and stereotypes and insensitivity to the needs of certain groups. Yet, the situation is more complex than that. The main reports of differential negative treatment from the young people were not in relation to persons in authority but to fellow students or people in public places, and they were not only in relation to white people. What we found was a complex nexus of tensions and hostilities – sometimes spilling over into violence – both between groups of Turkish-origin young people and across a range of ethnic groups.

7 No rush to settle: Turkish-speaking young people and marriage

Gill Jones (2002) suggests that the transition to adulthood is not a single but a triple process: from school to work; from parental home to own home; and from family of origin to setting up one's own family. The lengthening of the economic transition clearly has effects on the other two: young people are taking longer to reach the level of income to enable them to buy their own home and start having children. Young men, in particular, are remaining longer in the parental home and their economic dependency on their parents has lengthened. Is this true for the young Turks? Minority ethnic groups may have their own patterns of family formation: for example, young South Asian women in Britain experience considerable pressure from parents to marry in their twenties while many African-Caribbean young women have children in their teens and early twenties before starting on higher education and career formation (Fenton *et al.*, 2001).

As can be seen in Table 17, Turkish-speaking young people do not seem to rush into marriage or cohabitation. None of the people who are younger than 18 is married or cohabiting. Moreover, only 14 per cent of the 18 to 20 year olds are in this category. In fact, only 27 per cent of people older than 20 are married or cohabitating. (Cohabitation was not common: only 11 young people were cohabiting out of the whole sample.)

In that sense, the important factor in relation to marriage is therefore age. The young people did value marriage and having children but thought that it was a big responsibility and should not be rushed into. In other words, like their attitudes to their employment, the young people do not seem ready to settle down in terms of starting a family either. The young people, regardless of their gender, seek economic security before entering into this sort of commitment, like Cahide, a Cypriot female:

> I don't want to get married until the age of 30 anyway and then of course I would like a family but before that I want to work and earn my own money and you know hopefully buy a house.

Table 17 Marital status by age

	Single (%)	Married/cohabiting (%)	*N*
16–17	100	–	30
18–20	86	14	172
21–23	73	27	48
Total	85	15	250

This is more or less true for both sexes. Eighty-nine per cent of males were single compared to 77 per cent of females. Nor was there much difference between ethnic groups, with the Kurds least likely to be married/cohabiting (10 per cent) and the mixed group most likely (21 per cent).

The interviewees' attitudes towards relationships with the opposite sex were interesting. Almost all of them had girlfriends or boyfriends but some did not like to admit it too openly, since they do not like to be a 'gossip item' in their communities. Bengi, a Kurdish female:

I have a boyfriend. But nobody knows. It's not pressure, but rather I see from my cousins, it is people are sort of gossiping.

However, both females and males had a sense of how far one could go in their relationships. Most of the young people did not think it was acceptable to have a sexual relationship before marriage, but were in favour of 'harmless flirtations' before serious engagement with somebody. As Hasan, a Kurdish male said:

It's quite natural and normal for a female to have boyfriends as much as me having girlfriends. But, everything must be within the boundaries. A female can go with a male, but shouldn't be seriously involved.

Yet, some of the males said that they did not mind if their girlfriends had prior sexual relationships, like Baris, a Cypriot male:

Things are changing all the time now. It used to be like that, like a female wouldn't be able to go out with no one till she just married someone, the first time. But now everything's changing.

We found that inter-ethnic marriage was not at all common, even non-existent among the females, while only four of the married males had partners from outside the Turkish-speaking origin communities. Duygu, a Turkish female who has a Turkish boyfriend, said that:

It *[having Turkish boyfriend]* is important for me. Because, if things become more serious such as engagement or marriage, two families getting together well is very important for me. That's why.

However, some of the young people put more emphasis on religion than ethnicity in relation to their partner – like Nazim, a Turkish male:

> I prefer a Muslim *[even if]* with a different ethnic background, because, in the end, we are going to live in the same house *[have to live by the same rules]*.

The number of people who met their partners through their families or relatives is relatively high. This might also explain why the young people were more likely to have intra-ethnic marriages. On the other hand, they wanted to choose their partner themselves and have the final say like Ogun, a Turkish male:

> She *[his future wife]* should be Turkish. I mean, if she is one of the females from our village, even better for my family. Of course I don't agree with them. If up to them, I might marry tomorrow, but it's not me.

In fact, although they seemed to value their families' opinions in relation to their partner's ethnic or religious background, the young people were not in favour of an arranged marriage. The families' involvement in the young people's marriages does not suggest an adherence to arranged marriages in any strict sense. Alpay, a Turkish Cypriot male, replied to the question whether or not he favoured arranged marriages thus:

> No! I don't think so. I mean maybe the old-fashioned ones like my Nana and Dada but not me.

The young people who found their partners through family connections insist that their families did not intend to introduce their partners for marriage; rather, they met with their partners at some family gathering such as weddings. For instance, Sibel, a mixed-origin female, talked about how she met her husband:

> My cousin introduced us. He is a far relative. We liked each other and, when we told our parents, they were happy as well. They know each other, but never thought that we might like each other.

In fact, all the families we interviewed strongly disagreed with arranged marriages. The fathers of two females (one Turkish and one Kurdish) said that they would be happy with anybody who their daughters fell in love with. On the other hand, the families often also underlined that they trust their children not to do the wrong thing or choose somebody unsuitable. It seems that there is an unwritten contract between parents and children in relation to this issue. For instance, a Cypriot mother insisted that she did not mind her daughter's chosen partner, but then added that, if her daughter chose a Greek Cypriot male, her own father (the girl's grandfather) would turn in his grave because of the history between Greek and Turkish Cypriots. Yet, she did not believe that her daughter would do such a thing, since she is well aware of her mother's sensitivities.

In this chapter, several important features emerged in relation to the transition to independent households. First, the young people were not rushing to be independent. Second, while having a boyfriend/girlfriend was not unusual, sex before marriage was disapproved of in the main. Third, the young people usually thought in terms of independent family lives based on marriages, rather than cohabitation or single households. In this sense, they preferred to make a marriage commitment and to have children well after their eighteenth birthdays. Fourth, inter-ethnic marriages were still rare among the Turkish-speaking young people. Finally, the families' involvement with the young people's partner choices was apparent, but did not seem to constitute arranged marriages.

8 Multiple identities and belonging

This chapter deals with the kind of identity and sense of belonging expressed by the young people. Our focus is on what was said about British, religious and ethnic identities as forms of self-identification. It is clear from research on ethnic minorities that many groups have a strong, albeit varying, sense of one or more minority identity; and that, increasingly, this does not prevent them from also having a sense of other identities, such as being British (Modood *et al.*, 1997). The aim here is to see what self-identities were current among the Turkish-speaking people.

We asked the young people in the survey to pick one or more identities from several options, which included Turk, Kurd, Turkish Kurd, British Turk, British Kurd, Cypriot, Turkish Cypriot, Middle Eastern, Muslim, Christian, British, Atheist and, finally, Alevi. As can be seen from Table 18, the young people do not tend to use British as an identity. Sixty-eight per cent of the females and 75 per cent of the males chose only other identities for themselves.

As we expected, there is a strong relationship between being born in this country and choosing British as an identity. Table 19 shows that 84 per cent of the young people who were not born in this country did not think of themselves as British.

However, during the interviews, we found that having British as an identity was more complex than just being born in this country, explaining why more than half of the young people who were born in Britain did not choose a British identity either. This was not necessarily because they rejected the idea of being British *per se*. Rather, during the interviews, it became clear that there was a narrow and a wide meaning of 'British' being used. For some, 'British' meant the possession of a passport. An extension of this narrow meaning is that people are British if they live in Britain, as found in the quote below, which also introduces a wider, cultural or ethnic meaning of British. Ebru, said that:

> I don't feel I'm British. I am British but – well, everyone's British that lives here, but British to me is English. Real English people, to me.

Table 18 British as an identity by gender

	Using British only (%)	British + other ID (%)	Not using British (%)	N
Female	5	27	68	78
Male	1	23	75	171
Total	2	24	73	249

Data missing in one case.

Table 19 British as an identity by British born

Born in Britain	Using British only (%)	British + other ID (%)	Not using British (%)	N
Yes	6	42	52	86
No	1	15	84	163
Total	2	24	73	249

Data missing in one case.

Or as Firat, a Kurd, expressed it:

> I don't think it's something to do with me, because we are very different culturally. That's why I never feel myself a part of this country. With a British passport, you can have a right to live in this country. That's all. I mean I'm not English. There are people like blacks who are born in this country and think themselves English. But I think an English is more English than others.

Leyla, too, said that she did not feel British because she was not properly English:

> ... if I could say that I speak English like my first tongue, know English history very well and defend English ideas, then I might say I feel British. But I don't have this sort of things, so I can't feel being English.

This marks a much greater reluctance to think of themselves as British than that of Caribbeans and Asians, as found in the PSI Fourth National Survey (1994, reported in Modood *et al.*, 1997), where a clear majority thought of themselves as British, including many who were not born in Britain. The reluctance to consider mixed marriages, discussed in the last chapter, is another marker of a strong sense of community segregation.

On the other hand, not having British as a self-identity does not mean that the young people chose only Turkish as an identity. Indeed, nearly 60 per cent of the young people chose multiple identities for themselves. In fact, only 22 per cent of the males and 15 per cent of the females chose only Turkish as a self-description. While this is partly because of many Kurdish people's alienation from a Turkish identity (see below), it is still the case that the majority of the young people picked more than one identity, like Baris:

> I'm Turkish. Turkish Cypriot I guess ... I've got a British passport so I have to say I'm British. I was born in England but I don't say I'm English ... I do feel British ... I've got used to everything in England now, so just the way they work, the tax and everything. So I say I'm British.

Like British identity, Turkish identity was understood by many as an ethno-cultural idea. As can be seen in Table 20, more than half of the Kurdish young people did not identify as Turkish at all, while 44 per cent of Turkish young people used only Turkish identity. During the focus group discussion, Kurdish young people, for instance, said that they did not like to be called 'Turkish' at the school or in the street. One girl said:

> I did not mind if they call me somebody from Turkey. That might be all right. But I don't accept to be Turkish just because I came from there.

Religious identity does not seem to be central. Less than 5 per cent chose religion as their only identity. Sixty-eight per cent did not subscribe to a religious identity at all. This low use of a Muslim identity is, again, very different from the findings of the Fourth Survey, in which, for example, an overwhelming majority of Pakistanis and Bangladeshis said their religion was an important feature of their self-description and the way they lived their lives (Modood *et al.*, 1997).

Nevertheless, religious identity does seem to have an importance greater than suggested so far. The failure to choose Muslim as an identity may partly be because, for some of these Turkish-speaking young people, being Turkish or Kurdish or Turkish Cypriot already included a sense of religious belonging. Being Muslim was indeed seen by some as a cultural identity rather than as a religion. As Cahide, a Cypriot who did not pick Muslim as an identity, explained:

> My dad wanted me to grow in the Turkish culture and that's why he took me to Turkey, so I guess it is important for me to be Turkish but it's not that important to be a Muslim, no, I mean we are Muslims but we don't practise it, we don't practise the religion but we don't go against it either.

Table 20 Ethnic identity by ethnicity

Born in Britain	Only Turk as ID (%)	Turkish + other ID (%)	Not using Turkish (%)	N
Turk	44	46	9	99
Kurd	–	49	51	67
Cypriot	–	87	13	54
Mixed	21	48	31	29
Total	20	56	24	249

Data missing in one case.

The subscription to a religious affiliation as a cultural identity is a general phenomenon, seen among many Jews and also communities in, for example, Northern Ireland. Yet, it is interesting to find it among Turks, for Turkey is a multi-ethnic, multi-faith melting pot in which adherence to Islam co-exists with radical secularism. Yet, given the conflict on the island of Cyprus – in some respects, paralleling the divide in Northern Ireland – Muslim may have come to have a greater salience in the self-definition of Turkish Cypriots.

Yet, one implication of this indifference to religious identity and the seeing of religious identity as an ethno-cultural identity was an absence of a sense of identity with Muslims in general. When asked, 'do you think of yourself as a part of a larger Muslim community?', Ogun replied:

> No. I only feel myself Turkish. I mean I'm Muslim, but Muslim Turk.

For some, if you are Turkish speaking, you are assumed to be a Muslim – but not much of a Muslim; yet, being Turkish speaking is more significant than being a Muslim and is an important basis for solidarity. This might explain why two-thirds of the young people who pray and fast do not identify in religious terms; yet, on the other hand, a quarter of those who do not fast use a religious identity.

In relation to the young people's attitudes towards religion, we also discussed Islamophobia, the fear of, and hostility towards, Islam and Muslims. In general, Islamophobia did not seem to be a big problem for the young people. In fact, this term was not a familiar concept for them. Almost all of them needed further explanation of the term. Although they did not think that being Muslim was a reason for being discriminated against personally, they appreciated that it might be the case for other Muslims. For instance, Sinem argued that:

> I heard from the television that there are some negative feelings against Muslim people, but it is usually against Pakistanis. If I do not tell them I'm Muslim, they don't know. But I am sure that women with headscarves might feel different.

Some of them clearly thought that they had experienced more anti-Turkish than anti-Muslim hostility, like Murat, whose father is Kurdish and mother Turkish:

> I must say I suffered more when these killings happened in Turkey *[killings of two people in Istanbul after a football match with an English team]* than I did after September 11 … after the incidents in Turkey, I felt bit uneasy on the street for following couple of months.

Or, Ilhan, a Cypriot male:

> Yes, it is true. They say 'all Muslims are the same and terrorist'. But I never experienced anything against me, because nobody thinks I'm Muslim. Even my Pakistani friends can't guess that I'm Muslim. But I think after that match we struggled more, because, when English people came to kebab shops and when football was talked, the air became bit tense. But then I see the people shouted 'Bin Laden' at the girls with headscarves. But, again, since I have no beards or moustaches, I have nothing that sort against me.

In conclusion, we found that the young people were ambivalent about what it means to be British and reluctant to adopt that identity. Yet, at the same time, most did not simply use a Turkish identity. They usually choose multiple ethnic identities, but, in the majority of the cases, the term 'British' was not (yet) part of that plurality. This is complicated by the fact that the majority of Kurds refused to self-identify as Turks. Finally, the young people's relationship with religion is not straightforward. They do not consider themselves as part of a Muslim community, but rather, for some, their religious identity is a natural extension of their ethnic identity.

Box 3   Gulistan: on the way up?

Gulistan is a Turkish-Cypriot girl born in Britain and is third-generation Turkish with one younger sister. Both her parents had college educations and hold professional jobs related to the Turkish-speaking community. The family own their house.

Gulistan had no major problem during her education and got full support from her family, and received private tutoring during her secondary education. She said she did not experience discrimination during her education: her school was a mixed school and the staff were mixed as well. The staff always supported her and she had friends from various backgrounds.

While at school, she always worked in part-time jobs and, at the moment, she is working in an agency to make some money for her education. Before going to university, she had a gap year, because she needed to support herself financially at university, not wishing to rely on her family for everything. The work she did was always within the Turkish-speaking community.

Continued

Gulistan believes that her biggest advantage is that she can speak both English and Turkish, though she said that her Turkish is not that great. She can also use the internet and knows how to write letters.

She does not intend to marry at the moment or in the near future, as she wants to finish university first and find a good job. Gulistan is not concerned about her partner's origin as long as there is mutual respect. Religion is not an important part of her life. In relation to identity, she said:

> You can be a British Turkish Cypriot. British, because I was born here, I grew up here. I've been schooled here, I've made my friends here, I've worked here. But Turkish Cypriot, where my blood is, where my roots are.

9 Thinking positively: young Turkish-speaking people and the future

We have seen how disadvantage has shaped the lives of this group of young people. How do their experiences of life to date influence them? Despite their disadvantaged position, these young people are not pessimistic about their future. However, they have scaled down some of their expectations in the light of their difficulties. We asked the young people what they wanted to be when they were at secondary school. Though we were aware of the fact that most of the sample were answering the question as they remember it, still the comparison between their answers to this question and to the question about their present aspirations should show us how the early experiences of these young people affect their future perspectives. Table 21 shows that, when they were at school, more than eight out of ten of the young people wanted a professional job.

However, the number aspiring to get professional jobs is reduced to about half for the girls and just over a third for the boys after a couple of years of post-school experience. Most strikingly, when they were at secondary school, only about 10 per cent of them had no idea about their future. Now a quarter of the girls and a third of the boys are unsure where they might end up in ten years' time (Table 22). Gender differences were further apparent in that the boys were more likely to expect to be in unskilled/semi-skilled jobs, while the girls were more likely to expect to have professional jobs in the near future.

Table 21 Aspiration at school by gender

	Don't know (%)	Professional jobs (%)	Clerical/technician/ manual jobs (%)	N
Female	8	81	12	78
Male	12	83	5	172
Total	11	82	7	250

Table 22 Aspiration for the near future by gender

	Don't know yet (%)	Unskilled/ semi-skilled jobs (%)	Clerical/ office jobs (%)	Professional jobs (%)	N
Female	26	16	9	49	77
Male	33	25	5	37	169
Total	30	22	6	41	246

Data missing in four cases.

The majority, however, retain their optimism and their goals. They do not expect to be rich, but they want to have a comfortable life. When they were asked to describe their idea of success, almost all of them identified it with having a good job, house, car and a family, like Firat:

> Nobody can catch birds with his mouth *[it means everybody has some limitations, you cannot achieve everything]*. At the end, if you have a financial comfort and stability, if you can own a house and maybe own another one. I mean when you become old, you should manage to have a comfortable life.

However, self-employment, which has economically sustained the community so far, receives a mixed reception from young people. While they appreciated some of the advantages that self-employment might offer, such as being your own boss, they generally did not want to work for their parents. Murat, whose father has a kebab shop, argued that:

> I don't think the kebab shops have any future … In the near future, the big supermarkets like Sainsburys will start to open their chain of kebab shops and this will kill the business.

However, some of them think that, if you work hard and if your shop is in the area in which business is generally vibrant, you can still make money. Firat, who owns a shop together with his father and his uncles, explains:

> Considering the circumstances, this shop is the best business I could have. And, at the moment, my earnings are all right. Okay, I have to work seven days a week and God knows how many hours, but we don't have so many shops around here. So, overall, business is good.

Nevertheless, he said that he did not see this as his end goal, though he did see the future in terms of self-employment.

> Of course I don't think to do this job for long time. I just want to make some money and, if I can manage, I want to move into property business … Anyway, this is my Plan B. You can say a kind of escape plan.

It is clear that young people set themselves goals and have benchmarks, which are different from those of their parents. This is reflected in this passage from Ogun:

> I think the success is what our parents achieved, when they came to this country. If we go on with their business, it is not success for us. I think you must

be better than them. You should put more on whatever they achieved. At least, getting good education and finding a job in an English firm. I think this is achievement. What achievement for them is standard for me. I mean because any English born and grown up here can do what I say. Of course, not all English, but I can do it as well. I mean, this is my aim. Finding an employment in a big firm.

The young people appreciate that what their parents might regard as success does not equate with good prospects in Britain today. As Gulistan, a Cypriot girl with three A levels, pointed out:

I'm automatically successful in my family's eyes because I've gone to school, got my qualifications … I'm going to university, which probably isn't a big thing nowadays because everybody goes.

During the focus group discussions, we asked why they were so optimistic about the future. The young people, regardless of gender and ethnic background, thought that this country was still capable of offering many opportunities. They planned to compensate for their lack of qualifications by working long hours in their families' businesses in the future. The Cypriot young people looked on their parents' businesses as a fallback: they thought that, if everything else failed, they could still have a comfortable life like their parents. Kurdish young people remembered their experiences in Turkey and what they had been told by family members and other Kurds. They also looked at current media reports about Turkey, and the prospects for Kurds in Turkey, and concluded that nothing in Britain could be as bad as Turkey. Turkish young people expressed both of these opinions.

Nevertheless, it is remarkable that the Turkish-speaking young people have conventional views of success and are not pessimistic about their future, despite their many disadvantages and early experiences of the transition to adulthood. This, however, is a consistent finding in other recent studies of young people (for example, Fenton *et al.*, 2001; McDowell, 2002).

Moving on: beyond the enclave?

Despite all the difficult conditions in terms of employment, only 10 per cent of the young people would consider looking for a job outside London. Interestingly, though the young people did not think of moving to a different city, they were quite willing to move to a different country. Forty-six per cent of females and 37 per cent of males expressed the wish to work outside Britain. More than half of the mixed-origin and of the Cypriot young people would have liked to work in another country, compared to 29 per cent of the Turkish young people (see Table 23).

Table 23 Wish to work outside Britain by ethnicity

	Yes (%)	No (%)	N
Turk	29	71	99
Kurd	40	60	68
Cypriot	52	48	54
Mixed	52	48	29
Total	40	60	250

This does not mean that the other country they have in mind is Turkey or Cyprus. Indeed, they have a preference for a variety of western countries: the European Union, the USA and Canada are the most popular options.

It seems, then, that in the young people's mental map it is not just Turkey or Cyprus that may be nearer than Birmingham but also Dusseldorf, Paris, or even Los Angeles or Sydney. While South London seems quite distant to them, once they think about relocating, distance dissolves and New York seems as likely a candidate as Milton Keynes. This is probably not just the imagination at work. Given the extensive Turkish diaspora in the EU and other parts of the world, these young people may indeed know more about cities outside Britain than other cities in Britain, and may have more family members and others who can be of assistance to them outside Britain than they have in other parts of Britain. Their preferences for where they are willing to work may reflect realistic choices about possible relocation. If so, it may be that careers advice to Turkish-speaking young people needs to be more aware of the opportunities afforded by transnational networks as well as local niches.

10 Conclusions

This study has been concerned with a particular set of ethnic groups, those of Turkish-speaking origins, who are some among a number of 'invisible' minority groups in Britain. Such groups make little appearance in public debates about race relations and have been little studied within academic social science. These groups include, for example, migrant groups such as people from the former Yugoslavia and from the Soviet bloc states. This is partly because policy and research has focused strongly on those groups that are 'visible' in terms of being defined by their skin colour and that have been the more open victims of racism: African Caribbeans, Africans, Indians, Pakistanis and Bangladeshis. There is also a question of numbers and mobilisation, since certain groups who could be defined by 'colour' (for example, Filipinos, North Africans) have also been neglected and ignored: their numbers are less than those of the more visible groups and they have been less prone to set up their own political campaigning organisations to fight for civil rights. Yet, as this study has shown, the invisible groups may suffer from considerable levels of disadvantage.

This research has sought to uncover the distinctive experiences of Young Turks, Turkish Cypriots and Kurds, to illuminate the special problems they face and to give them a voice. We have highlighted some of the features of this invisible disadvantaged group and have noted that the Kurds, as the newest migrant group, suffer the highest levels of disadvantage in their lives. In part, this is linked to the refugee status that many of them have; while the longest settled group, the Turkish Cypriots, are the least disadvantaged. This pattern seems to be transmitting itself to the next generation. We offer several main conclusions along with some policy implications, which are sketched out in this final chapter.

We suggest that Turkish-speaking young people struggle to find their way in society because of structural disadvantages, exclusion and neglect, and that their transition to adulthood is not only prolonged and fractured, in common with the transitions of other young people, but also particularly constrained. While individuals respond to their situation in their own personal ways, nevertheless, the combined effects of racialisation, migration, ethnicity, gender and class continue to shape the lives of many young Turkish-speaking origin people and restrict their opportunities. Our research suggests that there are few agencies or organisations that specifically target these young people to assist them in the transition to adulthood, apart from their families and other community members.

Schools

Our interviews offered a bleak picture of the young people's experience of schooling. Most reported negative feelings; few were academically successful, nor were they particularly well prepared for the labour market. Rates of truancy and exclusion were high, especially among the boys. Teachers in areas of multiple disadvantage clearly have a hard job working to motivate children from deprived backgrounds. Ethnic tensions among the pupils make their job all the more difficult. However, it seemed to us that the schools had failed to grasp the specific situation of the Turks and Kurds and were not succeeding in making them feel included. For example, Enneli (2001) found that many young Turkish-speaking students carried out their work experience requirements within the Turkish community economy, thus losing a key chance to experience something of the wider economy. Little appeared to be done to address the problem of inter-ethnic conflicts and harassment among schoolchildren. Our respondents found lessons boring and new migrants, such as the Kurdish refugees, had language problems that were not addressed.

A useful strategy for local schools would be to employ more Turkish-speaking teachers who can help pupils feel that school is relevant to their needs. It would be helpful to focus on preventing inter-ethnic conflict, perhaps by employing somebody to mediate between different groups in schools or between students and teachers. Another possibility is to establish a special unit within a school for young Turkish speakers with behavioural problems, rather than simply excluding them from school. We believe that these recommendations may ease tensions in the schools and make the young people feel more secure and settled in school. This in turn might help to decrease the disturbingly high levels of truancy and exclusions. Schools also have a role in encouraging the Turkish-speaking young people to look outwards beyond their communities. For example, schools can encourage work experience and voluntary work with mainstream British firms and organisations.

Moreover, the research suggests that many parents are not at home with the British educational system. Although they try their best to support their children, they may not be knowledgeable about qualifications and their differing values; inevitably, they leave much to the school. Schools, therefore, should attempt to reach out to the parents about different options, providing them with more information about aspects of schooling and alternative career prospects. In this way, there can be a better partnership between schools and parents in supporting the young people and helping them to achieve their aspirations.

Careers advice

Young Turkish-speaking origin people are very dependent on their families, friends and communities for finding their first jobs. At the same time, they have high aspirations for future careers, which may be hard to fulfil if the first steps they take are wrong. They need more help in accessing available opportunities for jobs and training, and guidance in maximising their chances of attaining their chosen objectives.

The key agency here is currently the Connexions service, which has been charged with delivering an overarching youth advisory service for all young people aged 14–18. At the same time, Connexions has been assigned the responsibility of targeting groups that are considered to be most 'at risk'. Such designated groups include minority ethnic young people and refugees. It is not clear that Connexions is currently giving these young people the level of intervention they merit.

Young people have heard of the Connexions service in Haringey, unlike the New Deal or other schemes. During the focus groups they confirmed that personal advisers from Connexions had visited each secondary school and college in the area. As young people said, the PAs took their pictures and arranged Connexions identity cards, while, some time later, information about colleges was sent to their home. Yet, the young people were not aware of the fact that Connexions is an organisation designed to help vulnerable young people with all their problems and does not limit itself to being a careers advice service.

We learned of one useful temporary scheme in which a Turkish-speaking Kurdish PA had been seconded by Connexions to work in a refugee community centre. Schemes like this are to be commended and we would hope to see this kind of provision established on a permanent basis, since, as we have shown, young Kurds are the most disadvantaged of the three groups we studied, and are particularly at risk of falling into the NEET category. Young Kurds need special help with schooling and with overcoming the stigma they suffer as refugees and asylum seekers.

At the same time, we recommend that Connexions seeks to recruit PAs and mentors who are Turkish speaking to cater for these young people's needs. It may be useful to try to develop a mentoring or 'buddy' system within the borough, utilising minority ethnic young people who have been successful in schools. Research among other minority ethnic groups has highlighted the importance of positive role models. It is also important that good communication is established between school PAs, outreach PAs and the Connexions main office (which has proved to be a major structural weakness in the service in its initial phases) (Britton *et al.*, 2002; Coles, 2003).

Employment

Private employment agencies are, in theory at least, another possible source of help to broaden the employment horizons of these groups of young people, but their record is somewhat limited. The local private employment agencies usually offer low-skilled jobs, in a sense the British equivalent of the jobs available in the Turkish-speaking community, such as cleaning at airports or for big companies. The young people perceive these jobs as having poor working conditions and pay, and as being as insecure as their counterparts in the Turkish-speaking community. However, the agencies strongly believe that even young people with good qualifications should accept any job without complaining, since, as one agency employer put it, 'nowadays the market gives value to experience as well as qualifications'. There must be concern that the agencies are contributing to the formation of a low-wage, low-skilled youth economy: we should like to see them being more sensitive in matching jobs, various levels of qualifications and aspirations.

It may be preferable for local councils to take an active role in helping these young people into suitable jobs. In the case of Haringey, the ethnic composition of the council workforce does not yet reflect the borough's ethnic composition. The council has tried to encourage young Turkish-speaking people to apply for jobs in different departments without much success. In the focus groups, the young people said that they did not apply for these jobs because they felt they had little chance of getting them, given their lack of suitable qualifications and the language barriers. Some people were suspicious of public sector jobs in general. We suggest that councils attempt to target these groups more sustainedly and to employ outreach tactics to achieve targets. Such strategies have proved successful with other ethnic groups.

'Joined-up' help for the transitions

Our interviews also suggest that the councils need to embrace a holistic view about the problems of the Turkish-speaking young people, or indeed of their communities generally. The councils tend to organise departments in terms of their functions, not in relation to different communities they serve. This can create a divided and confusing system for some of these communities (and indeed for all young people who experience social problems). Young people need to contact different departments in order to get help with their various problems (such as housing, education and benefits). We endorse the 'joined-up' approach currently favoured within public policy. Inter-agency collaboration and identification of a 'key worker' to co-ordinate different agencies' roles is a major part of the Connexions' strategy (though it has proved hard to realise in practice). A similar approach may be needed in dealing with older young people (post-18) and could be a key objective of both state and voluntary agencies.

Another important principle of Connexions is consultation with young people in identifying initiatives and determining priorities. We suggest this principle be followed scrupulously by local authorities when considering the needs in the Turkish-speaking community. It is imperative that they should consult with these young people and act in harmony with the community organisations' own priorities. For instance, Haringey council has identified gang crime as a very important issue and has a section in the council dealing with it. When such arrangements are instituted, it is important that councils and other agencies liaise closely with the communities and establish partnerships with them to direct and monitor initiatives. Otherwise, there is a danger that the state activities may come to be seen as oppressive rather than sustaining, where a controlling and policing role may be perceived rather than a supporting and developing role.

In addition to the economic transition, the transition to independent households is important. The nature and characteristics of the young people's future independent lives, their identities and belonging, and their feeling towards British identity will shape the future of the community and their place in British society. Consequently, the agencies we mentioned above should not only concentrate on the young people's economic inclusion, but also be concerned to guide them and introduce alternative ways for them to interact and engage with wider society.

Increasing visibility: a place for Turkish-speaking origin people in a multicultural future?

Reiter and Craig (forthcoming) problematise the notion of citizenship in relation to young people in general. Where citizenship is commonly dependent on being employed, young unemployed people and young carers are in danger of being excluded from citizen rights. Reiter and Craig highlight that young minority ethnic people are especially vulnerable in this respect.

We have shown that Turkish-speaking young people are not pessimistic about their future and have conventional views of success – marriage, children, own home, a car and a good job or business. Moreover, they believe that such success is still possible for them in Britain despite their early experiences of adulthood. However, it is obvious that they perceive their community connections and families as a fallback and source of material support, if everything else should fail. This gives them security and may feed their optimism. But there is a potentially negative side here too and a need for policies to prevent these family cushions from becoming traps. The families and the community should not be relied on to guarantee a successful transition for these young people, and the young people should not have to depend on their families for support.

Schools, colleges, careers agencies and local government departments must, therefore, overcome their blindness towards the Turkish-speaking communities and develop an understanding of their needs. In the past, agencies have tended to concentrate their efforts on the more visible deprived minorities, such as the

Pakistanis, Bangladeshis and African Caribbeans. But, in this study, we have tried to show how young Turkish-speaking origin people are also among the most disadvantaged groups in multicultural London. We see this research as an initial step in raising awareness of the problems these young people face. More work is needed to explore the best ways to help them realise their potential so they can make a proper contribution to our economy and society. There is life beyond the kebab shops: Young Turks, Kurds and Turkish Cypriots deserve the chance to grasp their rights as equal citizens in an increasingly multicultural world. These rights are of two kinds (CMEB, 2000). First, there are the basic entitlements to the benefits of social, political and civil citizenship. Second, there has to be a recognition of difference and diversity. The 'invisibility' of young Turkish-speaking people suggests that neither set of rights is currently being adequately realised.

Notes

Introduction

1   It is difficult to find a suitable terminology to encompass the groups. 'Turkish-origin' is not quite right, because it does not cover those who are from Cyprus; nor is 'Turkish-speaking' because, for many Kurds, it is Kurdish, not Turkish, that is their primary language. If we use 'Turks and Kurds', this will omit the Cypriots. We do in fact use all three of these terms because no single term itself is satisfactory and nor is any other term. We mostly use 'Turkish-speaking' for the majority of the people studied, as their families do indeed speak some Turkish.

Chapter 4

1   Although this quote is not recorded, Hasan (not his real name) was willing for it to be noted. We gave him, like all the other interviewees, the assurance that we would not use his real name and that all information he gave us, including off-the-record notes, would be confidential.

References

Avrupa (2003) 'Avrupa eroini Turklerin kontrolunde', 24 July

Bates, I. and Riseborough, G. (eds) (1993) *Youth and Inequality.* Buckingham: Open University Press

Britton, L., Chatrik, B., Coles, B., Craig, G., Hylton, C. and Mumtaz, S. with Bivand, P., Burrows, R. and Convery, P. (2002) *Missing Connexions? The Career Dynamics and Welfare Needs of 16–17 Year-olds.* Bristol: Policy Press

Bynner, J. and Parsons, S. (2002) 'Social exclusion and the transition from school to work: the case of young people not in education, employment, or training (NEET)', *Journal of Vocational Behaviour*, Vol. 60, No. 2, pp. 289–309

CMEB (Commission on Multi-ethnic Britain) (2000) *The Future of Multi-ethnic Britain.* London: Profile Books

Coles, B. (2003) 'Connexions: an outbreak in purple and orange', *Benefits*, June

Enneli, P. (2001) 'Turkish-speaking young people in North London: a case of diversity and disadvantage', unpublished PhD thesis, University of Bristol

Enneli, P. (2002) 'Social exclusion and young Turkish-speaking people's future prospects: economic deprivation and the culturalisation of ethnicity', in S. Fenton and H. Bradley (eds) *Ethnicity and Economy – 'Race and Class' Revisited.* Basingstoke: Palgrave Macmillan

Fenton, S., Devadason, R., Bradley, H., Guy, W. and West, J. (2001) 'In and out of work: job changing, life changing and young adult identities', paper presented at International Sociological Association, Helsinki, August

Furlong, A. and Cartmel, F. (1997) *Young People and Social Change.* Buckingham: Open University Press

Hickman, M. and Walter, B. (1997) *Discrimination and the Irish Community in Britain.* London: Commission for Racial Equality

Jones, G. (2002) *The Youth Divide. Diverging Paths to Adulthood.* York: Joseph Rowntree Foundation

King, R. and Bridal, J. (1982) 'The changing distribution of Cypriots in London', *Etudes Migrations*, Vol. 65, pp. 93–121

Ladbury, S. (1977) 'The Turkish Cypriots: ethnic relations in London and Cyprus', in J.L. Watson (ed.) *Between Two Cultures: Migrants and Minorities in Britain*. Oxford: Basil Blackwell

Manco, U. (2001) 'Turks in Western Europe', unpublished paper at http: //allserv.rug.ac.be/~hdeley/umanco3.htm

McDowell, L. (2002) *Redundant Masculinities*. Oxford: Blackwell

McPherson, Sir W. (1999) *The Stephen Lawrence Inquiry. Report of the Inquiry by Sir William McPherson of Cluny*. London: HMSO

Mehmet Ali, A. (2001) *Turkish Speaking Communities and Education – No Delight*. London: Fatal Publications

Milliyet (2002) 'AB'de 82 bin Türk patron var', 30 December

Modood, T. (2003) 'Ethnic differentials in educational performance', in D. Mason (ed.) *Explaining Ethnic Differences*. Bristol: Policy Press

Modood, T., Beishon, S. and Virdee, S. (1994) *Changing Ethnic Identities*. London: Policy Studies Institute

Modood, T., Berthoud, R., Lakey, J., Nazroo, J., Smith, P., Virdee, S. and Beishon, S. (1997) *Ethnic Minorities in Britain: Diversity and Disadvantage*. London: Policy Studies Institute

Oakley, R. (1989) 'Cypriot migration to Britain prior to World War II', *New Community*, Vol. 15, No. 4, pp. 509–25

Onal, A. (2003) '_ngiltere'deki Türkiyeli topluluk üstüne bir çali_ma-1 ve 2', at <www.Gazetem.net>, 25 and 26 July.

Reiter, H. and Craig, G. (forthcoming) 'Youth in the labour market – citizenship or exclusion?', in H. Bradley and J. van Hoof (eds) *Youth, Labour Markets and Citizenship*. Bristol: Policy Press

Roberts, K. (1995) *Youth and Employment in Modern Britain*. Oxford: Oxford University Press

Robins, K. and Aksoy, A. (2001) 'From spaces of identity to mental spaces: lessons from Turkish-Cypriot cultural experience in Britain', *Journal of Ethnic and Migration Studies*, Vol. 27, No. 4, pp. 685–711

Sonyel, S.R. (1988) *The Silent Minority – Turkish Muslim Children in British Schools*. Cambridge: The Islamic Academy

Triandafyllidou, A. (2001) *Immigrants and National Identity in Europe*. London/New York: Routledge

Uras, G. (2002) 'Bitmeyen Goc', *Milliyet*, 24 October

Walby, S. (1997) *Gender Transformations*. London: Routledge

Appendix 1: The interviewees

Kurdish interviewees

Females

- Figen: she is 16 years old, born in Turkey, and came to Britain when she was 11. Her family are refugees. She is single and lives with her parents and sister in temporary accommodation. She has no GCSEs and is doing some GNVQ courses. She is working in an off-licence belonging to her uncle. The interview was conducted in Turkish in her home and not recorded.

- Leyla: she is Figen's sister. She has no GCSEs either and is currently doing a GNVQ course on computer studies, while working in a coffee shop. She has been engaged to a Kurd for one year. This interview was conducted in Turkish and recorded.

- Ceylan: she is 20 years old and married to a 22-year-old Kurd. She came to Britain when she was 11. She has been looking for a job for two years and is living in a council house with her husband. This interview was conducted in Turkish and not recorded.

- Bengi: she is single and 22 years old, and came to Britain when she was 16. She is living with her family in a council house. They are refugees. Currently, she is doing GNVQ courses in English and business, and also working in a coffee shop belonging to one of her relatives. This interview was conducted in Turkish and recorded.

Males

- Hasan: he is 17 years old and came to Britain when he was six. He is single and living with his family in their own house. The family was recently granted permanent residency. He is doing a GNVQ course and working in a shop for the time being. This interview was conducted in Turkish and recorded.

- Huseyin: he is 20 years old and came to Britain when he was 12. He has no GCSEs and is going to college to do GNVQ courses. He is also working in an off-licence. He is single and living with his family in a council house. This interview was in Turkish and not recorded.

- Dicle: he is 20 years old and came to Britain when he was 14. He is going to college and working in a kebab shop. He is single and living with his family in a council home. This interview was in Turkish and not recorded.

- Firat: he is 22 years old and came to Britain when he was 12. He is married without children and lives in a council house with his wife. He has no qualifications and currently works in a shop together with his father and his uncles. This interview was conducted in Turkish and recorded.

Turkish interviewees

Females

- Ayca: she is 16 years old and was born in Britain. She is single and living with her family in their own house. She has got nine GCSEs grades C and above. She is currently preparing for A levels and is also working part time in a retail shop. This interview was in English and recorded.

- Duygu: she is 18 years old and was born in Britain. She is single and living with her family in their own house. She has nine GCSEs grades C and above and also has three A levels. She is currently working part time in a retail shop. This interview was in Turkish and recorded.

- Sinem: she is 20 years old and was born in Britain. She has 11 GCSEs grades C and above and three A levels. She is looking for a job before going to university. She is single and living in her parents' home. This interview was in Turkish and recorded.

Males

- Mesut: he is 19 years old and was born in Britain. He has no qualifications and is looking for a job. He is single and living with his family in a council house. This interview was in Turkish and not recorded.

- Nazim: he is 19 years old and was born in Britain. He has no qualifications and is working in a retail shop. He is single and living with his parents. This interview was in Turkish and recorded.

- Ogun: he is 20 years old and was born in Britain. He has three GCSEs grades C and above and one GNVQ. He is working in his father's kebab shop. He is single and is living with his parents. This interview was in Turkish and recorded.

- Avni: he is 23 years old and was born in Turkey. He came to Britain three years ago with his Scottish wife. They are living in a council house and do not have any children. He is currently working for a construction company. This interview was in Turkish and recorded.

Cypriot interviewees

Females

- Cahide: she is 17 years old and was born in Britain. She has got seven GCSEs grades C and above and one A level in Turkish. She is currently preparing for her A levels. She is single and is living with her parents. This interview was in English and recorded.

- Ebru: she is 19 years old and was born in Britain. She has got five GCSEs grades C and above and three A levels. She is planning to go to university and is looking for a job. She is single and living with her parents. This interview was in English and recorded.

- Gulistan: she is 18 years old and was born in Britain. She has got three GCSEs grades C and above and three A levels. She is planning to go to university and is also working in a temping agency. She is single and is living with her parents. This interview was in English and recorded.

- Jale: she is 21 years old and was born in Britain. She has got nine GCSEs grades C and above and three A levels. She has a university degree in physiology but could not find a job and is now at college studying osteopathy. She is also working at her mother's sandwich shop. She is single and is living with her mother. Her parents are separated. This interview was in English and recorded.

Males

- Alpay: he is 16 years old and was born in Britain. He has got three GCSEs grades C and above. He is planning to go to college. He is single and is living with his family. This interview was in English and recorded.

- Baris: he is 19 years old and was born in Britain. He has got one GCSE grade C and two GNVQs. He is single and is living with his family. This interview was in English and recorded.

- Doruk: he is 20 years old and was born in Britain. He has got three GCSEs grade C and above and three A levels. He is going to university and is also working in his cousin's shop. He is single and living with his friends. This interview was in English and not recorded.

- Ilhan: he is 23 years old and was born in Britain. He has got one GCSE grade C and above and one A level in Turkish. He is married to a 21-year-old Turkish female. They do not have any children and live in rented accommodation. This interview was in Turkish and not recorded.

Mixed-origin interviewees

Females

- Aysegul: she is 21 years old and came to Britain two years ago. Her father is Kurdish and her mother is Turkish. She is an asylum seeker. She is currently going to college and working in a coffee shop. She is single and is living with her sister and brother-in-law. This interview was in Turkish and recorded.

- Inci: she is 18 years old and was born in Britain. Her mother is English and her father is Turkish Cypriot. She has got ten GCSEs grades C and above and four A levels. She is planning to go to university. She is currently working in a bank. She is single and living with her parents. This interview was in English and recorded.

- Sibel: she is 21 years old and was born in Britain. Her mother is English and her father is Turkish Cypriot. She has just finished at university and is working in a recruitment firm. She is married and living with her grandmother and her husband in a council flat belonging to the grandmother. This interview was in English and recorded.

- Oya: she is 20 years old and came to Britain one year ago. Her father is Kurdish and her mother is Turkish. She is going to college and working in a kebab shop. She is single and is living at her uncle's house. This interview was in Turkish and not recorded.

Males

- Kaya: he is 19 years old and came to Britain when he was seven. His father is Turkish and his mother is Kurdish. He has got three GCSEs grade C and above and one GNVQ. He is looking for a job and attending college. He is single and is living with his parents. This interview was in Turkish and recorded.

- Murat: he is 19 years old and came to Britain when he was six. His father is Kurdish and his mother is Turkish. He has got five GCSEs grades C and above, two A levels and four GNVQs. He is working in his father's kebab shop. He is single and living with his parents. This interview was in Turkish and recorded.

- Ozgur: he is 19 years old and was born in Britain. His father is Turkish and his mother is Irish. He has got seven GCSEs grades C and above and two A levels. He is going to university and is working in a supermarket. He is single and living with his family. This interview was in English and not recorded.

Appendix 2: Difficulties with the Bangladeshi fieldwork

By the end of August 2002, it was clear that, despite considerable efforts, we were struggling to meet our target of 100 completed questionnaires from Bangladeshis.

We were willing to see if the situation improved by the end of September but it was looking highly unlikely that there would be enough returned questionnaires for any statistical analysis. To continue pursuing this line was very likely to have had detrimental effects on the rest of the project resources and timetable.

In early September, we made a decision, in consultation with Joseph Rowntree Foundation (JRF), that, unless a substantial number of the questionnaires distributed over the summer were returned by the end of September, we would have to abandon this part of the project. As there was no real improvement by this deadline, this part of the project was abandoned.

The total number of questionnaires distributed to Bangladeshi organisations and families was 123. We contacted 12 people for their help and also sought help from various organisations (12 in total). But, after all these efforts, we received only 15 completed questionnaires.